Advance Praise for *It's a Sprawl World After All*

This book is controversial, but a must read. Many studies are available that quantify problems of our sprawl development pattern. *It's a Sprawl World After All* centers on the least quantifiable, but arguably, the most important impact—-the loss of a sense of community. The author gives a hard-hitting warning that must be heeded if we are to have a civil future.

> — Parris N. Glendening, President, Smart Growth
> Leadership Institute, Governor, Maryland (1995-2003).

Sounding an impassioned call to action and offering thoughtful, common sense suggestions for repairing the damage we have inflicted on our landscape and our way of life, Morris has given us a useful addition to the growing body of anti-sprawl literature.

> — Richard Moe, President of The National Trust
> for Historic Preservation and author of *Changing Places*

Morris brings [many] influences together with solid, progressive thinking to draw a clear picture of the sociological damage wrought by sprawl – as well as presenting solutions and options in which we can all participate.

> — From the Foreword, by Ray Oldenburg, author of
> *The Great Good Place* and Professor Emeritus of Sociology
> at The University of West Florida

In this cautionary tale of a landscape stretched to its limits, *It's a Sprawl World After All* simply yet eloquently illustrates how ~~b-urban sprawl has fractured social relationship~~ disappearance of civic-mindedness. Stra~~i~~ ing, Morris presents a book that is f~~a~~ account of the negative effects of spr~~.~~ mistic and pragmatic spirit aimed at ~~... ..he~~ virtues of walking, public engagemen~~t~~ ~~..~~mmunities.

> — Andy Hamilto~~n~~ ~~...~~dent, America Walks

In his compelling book, Doug Morris poses serious questions that beg for immediate answers from each citizen who has concerns about the quality of life in our increasingly unstable, disconnected, and hostile society.

— Leslie Charles, author of *Why Is Everyone So Cranky?*

In *It's a Sprawl World After All*, Doug Morris shows how sprawl has reduced our overall quality of life and turned neighbors into strangers. Most importantly, he offers practical suggestions on how readers can create meaningful, fulfilling connections in their communities – regardless of where they live. Read it and reap the benefits.

— Sam Horn, author, *Tongue Fu!* and
Take the Bully by the Horns

It's a Sprawl World After All reveals a litany of frightening details about America's failing economic, community and personal health; all tied to the unbearable auto dependency associated with our suburban and urban wasted places. As a people and as communities we require a collective thump on the noggin. We need to rethink how we are building our nation. This book helps us do that.

— Dan Burden, Director, Walkable Communities

Mr. Morris offers readers a passionate and exhaustive critique of all that is wrong with the nation, along with a common sense course for individual and community action.

— Helen Tangires, author, *Public Markets* and
Civic Culture in Nineteenth-Century America

With his engaging account of the American society's devolution, Douglas E. Morris has delivered a book that belongs in the town-planning canon alongside *Suburban Nation* and *The Geography of Nowhere,* and kindred volumes.

— Michael Dolan, author,*The American Porch:
An Informal History of an Informal Place*

It's a
SPRAWL WORLD
After All

It's a
SPRAWL WORLD
After All

Douglas E. Morris

NEW SOCIETY PUBLISHERS

Cataloging in Publication Data:
A catalog record for this publication is available from the National Library of Canada.

Cover design by Diane McIntosh. Girl on bench image: Getty Images.

Printed in Canada. First printing September 2005.

Permissions:
Figures 1.1-1.3 and A.1-A.3: Courtesy of the Frances Loeb Library, Harvard Design School
Figure 2.1: Courtesy of the Orange Empire Railways Museum, Perris, California (www.oerm.org)

Paperback ISBN: 0-86571-546-7

Inquiries regarding requests to reprint all or part of *It's a Sprawl World After All* should be addressed to New Society Publishers at the address below.

To order directly from the publishers, please call toll-free (North America) 1-800-567-6772, or order online at www.newsociety.com

Any other inquiries can be directed by mail to: New Society Publishers
P.O. Box 189, Gabriola Island, BC V0R 1X0, Canada
1-800-567-6772

New Society Publishers' mission is to publish books that contribute in fundamental ways to building an ecologically sustainable and just society, and to do so with the least possible impact on the environment, in a manner that models this vision. We are committed to doing this not just through education, but through action. We are acting on our commitment to the world's remaining ancient forests by phasing out our paper supply from ancient forests worldwide. This book is one step toward ending global deforestation and climate change. It is printed on acid-free paper that is **100% old growth forest-free** (100% post-consumer recycled), processed chlorine free, and printed with vegetable-based, low-VOC inks. For further information, or to browse our full list of books and purchase securely, visit our website at: www.newsociety.com

New Society Publishers   www.newsociety.com

To my loving parents, Don and Denise Morris, who were called away before the main event. Two seats remain empty.

Contents

Acknowledgments

OF ALL THE PEOPLE WHO HELPED this book become a reality, my parents, Don and Denise Morris, are definitely the most influential. Without their courage to raise a family overseas I would never have accumulated the international experience necessary to make the cross-cultural comparisons that are so fundamental to the insights presented in these pages.

The most significant primary sources for this book include Tom Knowles, Director of the Federal Bureau of Investigation's (FBI) Violent Criminal Apprehension Program (VICAP), who offered invaluable insights into the minds of serial offenders; Ray Oldenburg, Professor Emeritus of Sociology at the University of West Florida; Richard Moe, president of the National Trust for Historic Preservation; and Robert McNulty, president of Partners for Livable Communities.

I am indebted to a focus group of nearly 60 individuals — too many to mention here by name — who helped me craft the title for the book.

Then there are my writer friends who took the time to perform a final edit of individual chapters. Thank you Laura Collins, Brian McArthur, John Menditto, Eric Olsen, Pete Quesada, and Dianne Readman.

Innumerable influences contributed to the evolution of this book including a report I did for Ron Doberan's class at Notre Dame International (NDI) in Rome, Italy about the prevalence of serial killers in American life. The next influence was when my brother Dan returned from college one summer to our home in Denmark filled with stories about how America had allowed its public transportation systems to be put out of business by automobile and oil companies. Then along came Lori Gillen who dragged me to a pair of graduate courses at George Washington University. One class focused on the history of urban planning in the US; the other was a course in sociology offered by Amitai Etzioni, whose ideas about the importance of community are woven into the fabric of this book.

After that I spent two decades searching the US for the types of livable, community-oriented places I had known in Europe. My failure to locate such places in America prompted me to begin researching why they did not exist. Ten years into this investigation, my cousin Eric Olsen convinced me that I needed to put my ideas down on paper. After that process started, six very patient women spent countless hours listening to me refine my ideas. Thank you for your attention Katie Donahue, Karyn Denniss, Marlene Kweskin, Julia Rota, Linda Croke, and Karin Smith. Without you, this book would never have become a reality.

In terms of editorial assistance, the first to knead the book into shape was the aforementioned Julia Rota, and much of the section on incivility exists as a result of her suggestions. *Grazie* Julia! Next were Barbara Osgood-Hartness, owner of Poncha Press and Holly Hammond, a superb free-lance editor. Finally, Murray Reiss's editorial expertise helped shape the book into its final form.

I would be remiss if I neglected to mention Brother Joseph Zutelis at NDI, who taught me how to express ideas and create images through words. Though I never made it onto his wall of fame, without his tutelage this book would never have become a reality.

For all of these people, and for those I may have inadvertently neglected to mention, from the bottom of my heart, I thank you.

Foreword

By Ray Oldenburg, author of *The Great Good Place,* and
Emeritus Professor of Sociology at The University of West Florida

Adolf Ciborowski, who oversaw the reconstruction of
Warsaw after World War II, observed that in modern
times a third kind of destruction of cities has been added
to nature and warfare. We now destroy cities and towns in the
process of building them. That process, he added, seems creative
and progressive in principle, but the results are disastrous to the
well-being of the people. Nowhere are those results more obvious than in the United States, where New York's Ada Louise
Huxtable observed the "death of the city by development."

Destruction by development proceeded apace after World
War II, and when Lyndon Johnson became president in the early
1960s, he remarked that "greed and stupidity" guide urban
development. In his book *My Hope for America,* he wrote, "in the
next forty years we must rebuild the entire urban United States."
Attention had already turned to the plight of our inner cities and
in 1949 Urban Renewal was launched as the federal government's
scheme to combat poverty, crime, out-migration, a declining tax
base and a host of other inner-city problems. Results were not
heartening and Urban Renewal was followed by Community Action
Programs, then Model City Programs, then Community Development Block Grants, then Urban Development Action Grants,

then Enterprise Zones, and Empowerment Zones, each time with more money but less fanfare and less hope of remedy.

The peoples' response throughout was to continue to flee the city, and before long, America became the world's first and only suburban society. More people now live, have offices, find jobs, do their shopping, attend schools and colleges in the suburbs than in the cities. Initially, the term "white flight" was applied, but by the mid-1990s, Atlanta had half a million African American suburbanites, DC had more than that, and Los Angeles had almost that many. By 2010, it is predicted, 43 percent of the nations Hispanic's will live in the suburbs.

The new juggernaut of suburban development is characterized by low density land use, heavy reliance on automobiles, the absence of city centers, and, due to the vast areas encompassed, an infrastructure so expensive that stately public buildings and other urban amenities are not affordable. Social scientists variously referred to the phenomenon as "spread," "sprawl" and "scatterization." Eventually, sprawl came to be recognized as a far more pressing problem than those plaguing the inner cities.

Most previous books on the subject of sprawl cover the broad range of problems it presents. Air pollution, the destruction of green space, school crowding, infrastructure decline, the concentration of poverty, inadequate accessibility, depletion of natural resources, and the decline of community life are the main themes addressed in treatises on sprawl. Inclusion of the many, however, has a diluting effect upon specific concerns, and there is a need, well met in *It's a Sprawl World After All,* to focus on the social consequences of sprawl – on the kinds of human beings we have become as a result of it. That need is as compelling as its confrontation is overdue.

In reporting on the behavioral consequences of sprawl, Douglas Morris is performing a service which mainstream sociology declined. The discipline did not overlook the problem, so much as it denied its existence. In 1965, well after President Johnson had deplored the urban condition in America, one of sociology's leading lights proclaimed in *The New York Times* that we must "root out of our thinking" the idea that the physical form of communities has social consequences. Another prominent sociologist chastised the remarkably insightful and observant Jane Jacobs for promoting what he called the "myth of physical determinism."

Mainstream sociology also obscured the destruction of community that has been ongoing since the 1950s. Whether bulldozed away as "social debris" under Urban Renewal, or stillborn in sterile postwar subdivisions, communities no longer exist for the majority of our population. Sociology "rescued" community by insisting that a superior form of it had emerged, the "liberated community," wherein one was no longer tied to the place of residence. It's also called the "network" and the whole of it consists of a "focal individual" and the sum of his or her various connections with others. To call something that small, unstable and vulnerable a community is dubious sociology at best.

The importance of the present volume is that it exposes the deleterious social consequences of bad urban planning to which social scientists were largely inattentive. Indeed, it may be said that social science gave license to the politicians and developers who have wreaked Ciborowski's third kind of destruction upon our towns and cities.

Mr. Morris has written a good many books, which have received five-star reviews and which have demanded clear, accurate and thorough treatments of his subjects. He is an astute observer of people and places, and his powers of observation relevant to this book have doubtless been sharpened by the fact that he lived more than eight years in Italy, the country which Bernard Rudofsky identified as offering a "rearview mirror" of western civilization, and one in which towns and cities are built for people and their enjoyment of one another. Morris brings these influences together with solid, progressive thinking to draw a clear picture of the sociological damage wrought by sprawl – as well as presenting solutions and options in which we can all participate.

Introduction

> The aim should not be more goods for people to buy,
> but more opportunities for them to live.
> — Lewis Mumford

Despite our economy's current volatility, the majority of Americans are still better off financially than much of the rest of the world. Most of us have everything we could ever want or need — nice homes, good jobs, paid vacations, cars, televisions, stereos, computers, closets bursting with clothes, sporting equipment, major appliances, garages filled with tools, and well-stocked refrigerators. However, even with all of this wealth, something fundamental to human happiness is missing from our lives. In spite of all our possessions, entertainment options, and economic opportunities, many Americans still feel alienated, isolated, and alone. We lack all that suburban sprawl has eliminated from our lives: the safety, sense of belonging, and quality of life that come from living in genuine communities.

After residing in Europe for over 12 years, I am well aware of how vibrant small towns or city neighborhoods can enhance one's quality of life. For example, one of the places my family lived was the typical British small town of Northwood outside of

London. I can still remember times when my Mom would send me to go pick up a forgotten food item from one of the small stores lining the main street. Along the way I would exchange greetings with people I knew and smile at those I did not. I'd window-shop at the toy store, mess around with friends I ran into, barely remember to get the item requested, and much to my mother's chagrin, get home well past the designated time.

This could not happen in American suburban sprawl. Everything is so spread out now that such freedom is impossible; a car is required to get anywhere, and then when we arrive at our destination, after having passed thousands of people, we are still surrounded by strangers. Unlike life in the small towns and suburban villages of Europe, living in sprawl is an oppressively anonymous existence.

The United States used to be a nation of small towns, but since the end of World War II our towns have been torn down, paved over, or killed by a nearby mall or shopping center. What remains is considered "progress." Because of sprawl, towns similar to Northwood, and the commensurate quality of life they embody, are extremely rare in America.

Suburban Sprawl, Isolation, and Violence

A field of study called environmental psychology has established a clear link between the places where people live and how they behave. These findings bolster the understanding that in the short period of time since its emergence in 1945, suburban sprawl has transformed America from "one nation, indivisible" into a polarized and fragmented society. Secluded in our suburban homes, we now live in a society of strangers.

Communities once held our nation together, both physically and spiritually, helped keep our children safe, and offered us a sense of belonging rooted in a sense of place. However, in the 60 years since suburban sprawl became the dominant urban setting, American society has not only mutated into something alienating and uncivil, but it has become oppressively violent as well.

This has resulted in an environment of fear that reduces everyone's sense of well-being and safety. Contrary to popular mythology, violence in America is not limited to inner cities. This reality was exposed by the series of tragic school shootings that occurred in Littleton, Colorado; Jonesboro, Arkansas; Conyers, Georgia; and other suburbs across America, including: Springfield, Oregon; Carrolton, Georgia; Paducah, Kentucky; Santee, California; Philadelphia and Hattiesburg, Mississippi; and Red Lion, Pennsylvania.

These events are only the tip of the iceberg. As reported in *The Washington Post,* violence in all its forms has become so omnipresent that Americans no longer feel that they can escape its threat by moving to the suburbs.[1] Commenting on the gunman who killed two people in Seattle on November 3, 1999, the day after a similar tragic event occurred in Hawaii, President Clinton summed up the situation by saying, "I don't think we understand just how much more violent the United States is than other countries."[2]

Statistics clearly show that by a wide margin more murders, rapes, and serial killings are committed in the US per capita than anywhere else in the world. One example of this disparity in levels of violence was reported by *The Washington Post:* "In 1995, handguns were used to kill 2 people in New Zealand, 15 in Japan, 30 in Great Britain, 106 in Canada, 213 in Germany, and *9,390* in the United States (emphasis added)."[3] With statistics like these, it's surprising that Kevlar, the fabric that bulletproof vests are made from, is not woven into everyday clothing in America.

America's oppressive levels of violent behavior create a pervasive sense of foreboding that permeates the very essence of everyday life. Women are afraid to take walks at night, even in their own neighborhoods. Parents no longer let their kids go to the park or playground alone. Most of us consciously or unconsciously alter what we do, or what we allow our children to do, to protect ourselves from the society in which we live.

This situation emerged so slowly that most of us are not even aware of its existence. We are all like the proverbial frog in the pot of water that is gradually being brought to a boil. If you drop a frog into hot water, it instantly leaps out. But if the water is slowly heated, the frog remains unaware, unconcerned until it is too late.

Most of us never realize how dangerous America is until we remove ourselves from the heat of this society and visit another developed nation. A common theme running through many of the stories women tell me about their experiences in Europe is that they feel safe there. No matter where they have traveled, whether Italy or France, Denmark or Switzerland, American women generally described their experiences as powerfully liberating. One person said, "I felt as if a weight that I did not even know was there had been lifted off of my shoulders." That weight is the burden of potential victimization that women in America carry with them every day.

Living or traveling in the safe, community-oriented environs of Europe alleviated their fear, because in general in those countries there is little to fear. European societies are incredibly safe in comparison to ours. In fact, the Centers for Disease Control and Prevention (CDC) found that violence in America is at epidemic proportions, while in other first-world nations it is not.[4]

Being able to live without having to constantly look over our shoulder helps to make life much more fulfilling and enjoyable. Regrettably, America, which was once the land of the free, because of the alienation of sprawl, has now become the land of the frightened. Sprawl has turned neighbors into strangers, and strangers into threats.

Early Suburban Communities

America was not always like this. Before 1945, people lived in safe city neighborhoods that had not yet been bulldozed to make room for highways, or in small towns that had not yet been turned into strip malls. People felt connected to their towns and urban neighborhoods because those places still existed in a coherent, community-oriented form.

Suburban development prior to World War II, in contrast to the formless sprawled wasteland of today, was patterned after the successful and popular Garden City model (see Figures 1.1–1.3). This development philosophy created small towns that combined all the functions of life — schools, banks, stores, offices, restaurants, public transport, libraries, etc. — with housing for a variety of income levels and easily accessible public

Figure 1.1

FOREST HILLS, NEW YORK – ILLUSTRATION CIRCA 1915

Courtesy of the Frances Loeb Library, Harvard Design School.

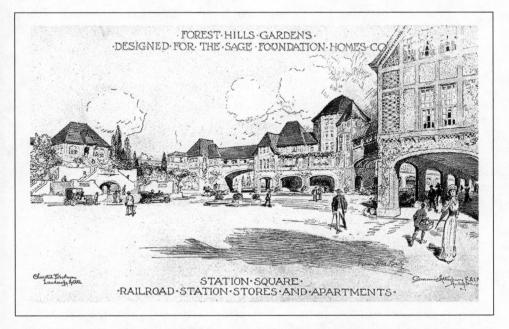

The Forest Hills Garden City-style suburban development combined stores, apartments, and homes, bringing people together to create a small town community.

transportation. Garden City-style developments continue to serve as the basis for urban planning in most of the world.[5] Through the end of World War II in America, Garden City developments were the norm, allowing for a sense of community to exist in these newly built suburbs.

Started in England by Ebenezer Howard, Garden City suburban small towns resembled English villages. The layout of these places encouraged multi-use development patterns, with light industry, stores, and public buildings located alongside housing and green space. Garden City suburbs provided each family with its own house and garden, and offered all the functions of life within easy walking distance of home. These well-designed suburban towns were connected to the city core, and to each other, by a variety of public transportation options that included rail as well as roads.

Garden City suburbs flourished all over America, creating places to live for all classes of society, and were developed as purposeful efforts to achieve a supportive and complete community.[6] These early American suburbs were well-planned and wonderfully livable, and they remain some of America's last surviving communities today.

Whereas people today equate suburban development with negligent planning and incompetent design, the Garden City suburbs had sophisticated layouts and distinguished designs. Many of these early suburbs have become synonymous today with livability, charm, and quality of life. They include Chestnut Hill in Philadelphia, Mariemont outside Cincinnati, River Oaks in Houston, Beverly Hills and Palos Verdes near Los Angeles, Coral Gables near Miami, and Forest Hills outside New York City (see Figures 1.1 and 1.2).

Garden City suburbs were by no means elitist, nor were they even exclusively middle class. In fact, many Garden City developments started off as public housing funded by the government. A fine example of this is Seaside Village in Bridgeport, Connecticut, constructed in 1918 with 257 dwellings in a village design. To this day it remains a quality, community-oriented

Figure 1.2

FOREST HILLS, NEW YORK – BIRD'S EYE VIEW, ILLUSTRATION CIRCA 1915

Courtesy of the Frances Loeb Library, Harvard Design School.

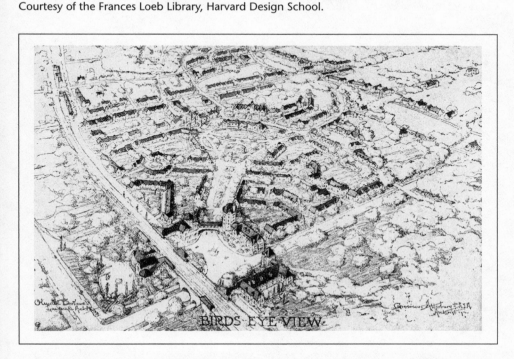

The Forest Hills suburban development created a small town by combining stores, public buildings, and residences, all within walking distance, and connected it to the surrounding area by public transport. Prior to World War II, this was how the majority of American suburbs were built.

place to live.[7] Another working-class development, Yorkship Village (see Figure 1.3), now known as Fairview, began in 1918 as a thriving neighborhood of a thousand dwellings near Camden, New Jersey. Today it still exists as a solid, mixed-use, mixed-income community, not far from its blue-collar roots.

The suburbs developed before World War II were built not only as investment opportunities, but were also created to enhance people's quality of life and sense of community. In contrast, the unplanned sprawl that exists today, where the functions

Figure 1.3

YORKSHIP VILLAGE PLAN, CAMDEN, NEW JERSEY

Courtesy of the Frances Loeb Library, Harvard Design School.

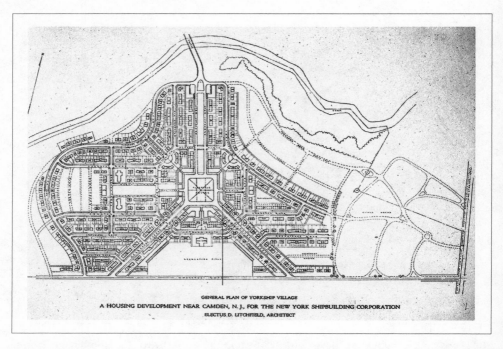

GENERAL PLAN OF YORKSHIP VILLAGE
A HOUSING DEVELOPMENT NEAR CAMDEN, N. J., FOR THE NEW YORK SHIPBUILDING CORPORATION
ELECTUS D. LITCHFIELD, ARCHITECT

A successful example of Garden City suburban development that integrates all the functions of life around a central village green. This town was designed and built for shipyard workers.

of life are scattered all over the landscape, promotes little but alienation and isolation. I challenge you to find a sense of community in a strip mall, shopping center, or suburban office park. Even suburban subdivisions, places where people live, are generally devoid of genuine communities. I have interviewed a number of suburban residents from all over the country who lament not knowing their neighbors despite living among them for years. Even if people do know one another, and a semblance of a community does exist, that sense of connection is dependent on those who instill it, rather than the place where the people live.

Once the individuals who act as the community catalysts move away, the sense of community they instilled leaves with them.

Considering Americans' adoration of small towns, the way our country has turned out is rather odd. Talk to anyone about what is quintessentially American, and more often than not, small towns feature prominently in peoples' hearts and minds. It is no accident, for example, that the Walt Disney Company creates classic, picturesque Main Streets in the hearts of its amusement parks. However, in the majority of places where we actually live, small town main streets have almost completely disappeared.

Automobiles

Despite Americans' veneration of small towns, without coherent national, regional, or even local urban development plans, our country has ended up as a sprawling mess. The functions of American life are zoned far away from one another, forcing people to live, work, and shop in widely dispersed locations, necessitating that they spend inordinate amounts of time in their cars. The automobile was once a symbol of freedom. Now it has become a prison.

A study conducted by the Sierra Club concluded that many Americans spend almost 15 hours per week in their cars.[8] Another study shows that the average American driver spends 443 hours each year behind the wheel — the equivalent of 55 8-hour days or 11 work weeks.[9] Whatever the numbers, whether it is commuting to work, making a run to the grocery store, drugstore, mall or church, or ferrying kids to parties, movies, soccer practice, cheerleading sessions, or friends' houses, we have become slaves to our automobiles.

How can we spend quality time with our families, or have meaningful relationships with our significant others if we spend more time in our cars than at home? When can we pursue those activities that would make our lives fulfilling if our time is wasted commuting or doing errands?

While automobiles are stealing our time, they are also monopolizing our space. In many of our cities, infrastructure to accommodate cars consumes between 60 to 70 percent of the landscape in the form of streets, parking space, and highways.[10] Maryland, no more automobile-dependent than any other state in the nation, has ten parking spaces for every car. All over the country, in cities where beautiful old buildings used to stand and neighborhood communities once thrived, parking complexes now exist. In suburbia, where bucolic small towns once flourished, oceans of parking lots surround ugly neon strips of commercial architecture.

While Americans continue to cede urban space to the automobile, Europeans have taken back large portions of their cities from cars, creating extensive pedestrian zones. They have also expanded already diversified transportation systems, reducing the need for automobiles, helping to retain attractive, livable cities and small towns. Anyone who has ever visited the Piazza Signoria in Florence, or shared the festive atmosphere of Strøget in Copenhagen, or strolled along the Corso Vanucci in Perugia knows something of the beauty of European urban communities.

Municipalities such as Paris, London, Amsterdam, Madrid, and Stockholm are all examples of beautiful and habitable European cities. Each has a different layout and design, but all are configured to benefit people and to enhance community. And each of these cities has well-preserved small towns on their outskirts connected to the city by extensive public transportation systems. This is the norm in Europe.

To be sure, European towns and cities have not always been paragons of urban planning. From the end of World War II until the mid-1960s, many European nations acted very much like America continues to, and allowed private interests to triumph over public good. In many cases, open collusion existed between municipal authorities and real estate developers. This resulted in huge swaths of land outside many large cities being given over to unplanned tracts of apartment buildings, such as those surrounding Naples and Palermo. Fortunately, most European nations quickly learned from their mistakes, cracked down on the corruption in real estate speculation, and began to plan their urban spaces more intelligently. Haphazard suburban development screeched to a halt, and extensive auto-free enclaves where people could gather and children could play without worrying about getting run over were implemented in virtually every European city and town. In downtown Rome alone, almost 500 acres have been turned into pedestrian areas.[11] In Venice, cars are completely banned.

As a result, simply walking down the street in nearly any European city or town is a safe and pleasant experience filled with the joy of community life. You see people arriving informally, greeting friends, doing their daily errands, going back to work, or just continuing to stroll. It is like watching a free-form community dance, filled with smiles, hugs, pleasant greetings, laughter, conversation, and pecks on the cheek. I travel to Italy frequently and spend much of my time sitting in piazzas or wandering streets, reveling in the embrace of being in a place where people know one another, and are friendly to strangers.

One community activity I particularly enjoy in Italy is the evening *passeggiatta,* the nightly stroll. In every Italian city and town, big or small, there is a place — and in larger cities, a number of different places — where residents go before and after dinner to commune with one another. In European cities and towns, people know one another; they are a part of each other's lives.

What Happened to America?

When I returned to the United States after living for twelve years overseas, I expected to find the same types of community-oriented towns and city neighborhoods I knew in Europe. I was saddened and shocked to discover that in the majority of cases my native land lacked such places. Much of what I had come to appreciate about life in other "first-world" societies simply does not exist in America.[12]

In an attempt to disprove this negative impression of my native land, I began a two-decade long cross-country search for genuine communities. I went from one coast to the other, visiting streetcar, railroad, and garden suburbs. I explored college towns, urban neighborhoods, rural hamlets, old company towns, greenbelt villages, suburban developments, strip malls, office parks, and every place in between. Although I found a few locations that had a semblance of what exists in Europe, my search confirmed that in the majority of cases the United States does indeed lack genuine communities — the necessary foundation for a safe and healthy society.

Jane Jacobs, renowned urban visionary, in her landmark book *The Death and Life of Great American Cities,* observed that before the advent of sprawl daily interaction on the sidewalks of cities and towns was the glue that held society together. But today in America, sidewalks are empty, and in many places they don't exist at all. In fact, most municipalities no longer have the central cores where sidewalks would even be useful. American "towns" today are gruesome boulevards of commerce, with garish fast-food outlets, huge big-box stores, monotonous office parks, cookie-cutter housing clusters, screaming neon signs, contrived themed restaurants, and roads choked with cars. Our urban spaces today are the direct opposite of what our society needs to be safe, livable, and community-oriented. In our frantic pursuit of progress, we have paved over the American dream.

As a nation we have achieved extraordinary technological, scientific, and economic gains, yet we are deficient in so many areas that would make life fulfilling and meaningful. We can explore outer space, yet we cannot build safe and livable communities. We have linked two oceans with the Panama Canal, but we have the least-developed passenger rail and public transportation systems in the developed world. We can map the human genome, yet our nation is a sprawled mess.

We have supermarkets and shopping centers filled with an endless array of products, but the people who wander in these places do not know one another. Our public existence is one anonymous moment after another. Despite all of America's advances, we have created an urban environment filled with lonely people. We have developed an economy that fulfills most of our material needs, but we live in a society where people lock themselves in their homes afraid of the strangers that surround them.

Hundreds of millions of Americans, over 70 percent of the population, reside in sprawl, unaware of the subtle and not-so-subtle ramifications of its presence in their lives. Most of us do not associate our feelings of loneliness, depression, and fear with our physical landscape. Being so ubiquitous, sprawl avoids detection by the general public as the root cause of many of our personal and societal woes. However, according to the many experts I will be referring to in the course of this book, it is becoming clear that our physical landscape has an irrefutably negative impact on human and societal development, health, and behavior. If we continue to ignore sprawl's influence, and neglect intelligent urban planning, every American's safety and quality of life will remain threatened.

We deserve to live in places where we can let our children explore the world around them without fear of them being snatched. We deserve to be able to walk the streets without worrying about being assaulted. We deserve small towns where we are recognized and feel a sense of belonging. We deserve well-designed communities that are more than just places on a map, but are also, more importantly, places in our hearts.

Read on and find out how you can either find such communities around where you live or create your own; how you can keep your family safe; and how you can fulfill the promise of the American Dream in the alienating expanses of sprawl. Join the millions of people taking charge of their lives, who are finding ways to counteract the human costs associated with living in suburbia.

CHAPTER ONE

Sprawl Versus Community

> We must stop talking about the American dream
> and start listening to the dreams of Americans.
> — Reubin Askew

A N ENTIRE FIELD OF STUDY, URBAN PLANNING, exists to help us
manage the built environment and keep our cities, towns,
and neighborhoods healthy, safe, and livable, while also
improving a sense of community and enhancing our economic
prospects. No urban plan is perfect, but plans need to be in place
to ensure a society's health and a community's well being.

Regrettably, after 1945 America decided to forego comprehensive urban planning and implemented a series of disjointed, disconnected, and destructive ideas that bulldozed entire sections
of American cities and eliminated small towns from the landscape. (See "Appendix A: How Sprawl Came to Be" for more
details about the history of suburbia.) Instead of preserving our
cities and helping them grow, our government embarked on
unproven initiatives that wiped out supposedly blighted urban
areas, historic buildings, vibrant neighborhoods, and the extensive communities located in and around them.

During this period, local officials were guided by imprudent national leaders, such as Alfred Bettman, the first president of the American Society of Planning Officials, who actively promoted the concept that existing urban areas should be completely eradicated, then rebuilt.[1] He, and others who shared his views and held the reins of power, felt that the beautiful old buildings and character-filled neighborhoods of American cities should be razed to the ground and redeveloped using modern building techniques and designs. The sad result of this misguided era in our nation's history is that once vibrant, livable, and safe American cities are now shells of their former selves. Instead of communities, our cities are desolate office parks. Instead of safe neighborhoods, there are war zones. Instead of livable places, we now have highways, parking garages, and empty lots.

While our cities were being leveled, the manner in which we built our suburbs changed radically as well. As mentioned in the previous chapter, pre-World War II suburbs were built based on the proven Garden City model, while the post-World War II era saw the rise of the development pattern now known as suburban sprawl, or sprawl for short.

Many now view the years from 1945 to 1955 as a Dark Age in our nation's urban history. Projects were undertaken and policies implemented that dramatically reduced the livability of much of our nation and the quality of life for most citizens. Our economy may have grown, but because of sprawl our sense of community and personal safety have been severely compromised.

What is Sprawl?

What exactly is suburban sprawl? What are the characteristics that define the places where over 70 percent of Americans now live? There may be slight differences in the form that sprawl takes throughout the country, but no matter whether it is outside Washington DC, Dallas, Miami, Minneapolis, Atlanta, LA, or Seattle, sprawl has several distinct and common characteristics:

1. **Low density design.** Sprawl is tens of thousands of physically autonomous residential subdivisions developed at low densities and spread over the landscape. Small towns are replaced by garish, neon-lit commercial strips strung along major traffic arteries.

2. **Lack of multi-use development patterns.** With no corner stores, cafés, restaurants, offices, public buildings, and homes within an easily walkable area, genuine communities in America have gone the way of the dodo bird.

3. **Automobile dependence.** With the functions of life spread all over the landscape, cars are the only practical mode of transportation in sprawl. Modern suburbs are built to accommodate cars and commerce, not people or public transit. Walking has been eliminated as a safe and pleasant means of locomotion. An overall lack of sidewalks and pedestrian areas effectively reduces foot traffic, eliminating the possibility of social interaction.

4. **Gridlock.** Subdivisions in sprawl are accessible by a hierarchy of feeder roads that offer few interconnected, alternative routes. These all disgorge traffic onto a few major arteries, which are quickly saturated by the volume of vehicles, causing gridlock.

5. **Inadequate public transit.** Mass transportation is scarce in sprawl, except for infrequent bus service along major arteries. Without public transportation hubs, generally train or trolley stations, around which small towns could develop, there are few community gathering places in sprawl.

Suburban sprawl, no matter how you look at it or where it exists, is a formless, centerless, fragmented urban structure that the Sierra Club calls "the Dark Side of the American Dream." James Howard Kunstler, best-selling author and world-renowned urban critic, describes sprawl as "a landscape of scary places, the geography of nowhere, that has simply ceased to be a credible human habitat."[2]

In Sprawlsville, as people go off to work in the morning or take their children to the school bus, some may wave, others may greet neighbors, but encounters such as these are rare. In many cases, people who have lived next door to one another for years do not even know each other's names. Even if there is some brief morning contact, after the commuters and school children depart, those that remain lock themselves tightly in their homes.

When the residents of sprawl do leave their fortresses, they need to use their cars to shuttle back and forth to widely dispersed supermarkets, fast-food outlets, office parks, and shopping malls. But these places, despite all the people in them, are not communities. No one lives in them. No one grows up or grows old in them. People simply wander in the presence of other wanderers. Connections are rarely made or sustained. People enter these places anonymously and usually leave without recognizing a soul. Then they drive back to their home, open the garage door using the remote control, and cocoon themselves.

Sprawl denizens live isolated inside their homes or behind the fences of their backyards, rather than mingling in public spaces with others. The main reason for this is that sprawl offers no convenient and pleasant places for people to gather. There are no main streets of local shops, restaurants, and cafés that people could stroll to in the evenings. All of this lessens the chance for human interaction to occur. Life in suburbia is the antithesis of community.

No One Walks Anymore

This loss of pedestrians is grave. The net effect of 280 million Americans driving everywhere is an increase in congested roads, polluted air, and obesity. It also contributes to a growing sense of isolation all over the country. Walking is considered by many experts to be the glue that holds communities and, by extension, society together. According to Ray Oldenberg, globally respected urban sociologist and author of *The Great Good Place* — a book about the importance of informal community gathering spots —

the number of amenities located within walking distance is a good measure of the health and vitality of an area. This distance is generally regarded as between half a mile to a mile.

Unfortunately, in America today almost nothing is within walking distance of where people live. As a result, most of us no longer walk anywhere, whether it is going to school or work, doing errands, or just taking a stroll. According to Sprawl Watch Clearinghouse and the CDC, the number of adults and children walking to work and to school has declined dramatically since the 1970s. Although walking used to be the most common way of getting around in cities and towns, today only 5.5 percent of all trips are on foot.[3] The death of American communities and the breakdown of our society is embodied in the lack of people walking.

Moreover, even the places where we could walk, such as the neon strips of adjoining shopping centers, discourage pedestrians. Each parcel of land is developed independently, with little or no physical, functional, or aesthetic relationship to neighboring developments. Huge surface parking lots isolate one building from the next, eliminating the possibility of walking. People are often forced to drive 100 feet to get to the next group of stores, instead of being able to stroll over to them.

Modern suburbs were built to accommodate cars and commerce, not people. As a result, people no longer walk, casual social interaction no longer occurs, and consequently, genuine communities no longer exist.

No Main Streets
In June of 1999 the National Trust for Historic Preservation (NTHP) placed America's "main street" at the top of its most-endangered-sites list. The NTHP has risen in prominence in the sprawl wars under the leadership of its president, Richard Moe, the author of *Changing Places: Rebuilding Community in the Age of Sprawl*.

Sprawl, according to Moe, robs Americans of the intangibles of community — neighborliness, civic beauty, a sense of belonging, and a shared experience of living in a unique environment. Says Moe, "I defy anyone to show me a sense of community in a strip mall."[4]

In a speech about sprawl given in 1996, Moe said, "You see fast-food outlets and office parks and shopping malls rising out of vast barren plains of asphalt. You see residential subdivisions spreading like inkblots, obliterating forests and farms in their relentless march across the landscape. You see cars, thousands of them, moving sluggishly down the broad ribbons of pavement or halting in frustrated clumps at choked intersections or parked in glittering rows in front of every building. You see a lot of activity, but not much life. You see the graveyard of livability."[5]

A country's physical landscape is literally and figuratively the foundation upon which its society is built. Two fields of study — psychogeography and environmental psychology — point out that many of a society's strengths and weaknesses can be traced to the quality of its urban design. The way we live our lives is determined by the physical landscape in which we reside. The way a society evolves is determined by the places where its people live. This is generally understood in other nations, but here in America it is not. By creating sprawl, we have ignored this most basic understanding of how to keep a society stable, safe, and healthy.

In the years since sprawl became the foundation of modern America, our society has crumbled. "It is no coincidence," writes Philip Langdon in *A Better Place to Live,* "that at the moment when the United States has become a predominantly suburban nation, the country has suffered a bitter harvest of individual trauma, family distress, and civic decay."[6]

Certainly, suburbia seemed like a good idea at the time — spacious homes, tidy lawns, cars in every garage, full refrigerators, and broad streets. But if you peel back the façade, sprawl is not so pristine and paradisiacal. On the outside, sprawl may look wonderful, but its core is devoid of any real life. At night in suburbia, after the roar of lawn mowers, the swish of water sprinklers, and the barking of lonely family dogs have subsided, all that is left is the ghostly cackle of sitcom laugh tracks or the faint roar of televised sporting events. Noticeably absent in suburbia is the hum of conversation that comes from a spontaneous community gathering. As a result, suburbia is almost completely devoid of the replenishing energy of community life.

Only Niche Communities

In the anonymous expanses of sprawl, people must go out of their way to be part of each other's lives. We cannot simply walk out the door and stroll a short distance to a gathering place and feel a welcome sense of belonging. In everyday suburban life, whether in our neighborhoods or doing errands, we are surrounded by strangers. In order to connect with others, we have to create formalized gatherings — what I call "niche" communities — such as book clubs, sports leagues, volunteer activities, neighborhood associations, and other organized activities or intentional events. Even meeting with our friends is a heavily formalized affair, something we have to plan weeks in advance to accomplish.

Indicating the deep psychological need for social interaction, many of us participate in several of these niche communities. Although they are meaningful in their own way, we do not live in these niche communities, so their potential for fulfillment is correspondingly limited. In healthier societies such as those in other developed nations, niche communities exist to complement, not take the place of, genuine communities.

In his book *The New Golden Rule,* Amitai Etzioni comments on the increasing prevalence of these niche communities, what he calls "quasi" communities, and how they reflect a decrease in overall social capital. An esteemed professor at The George Washington University, and former senior advisor to the White House, Professor Etzioni is founder and director of the Communitarian Network, a US-based interest group that publicizes the demise of and advocates for a return to community-oriented living. He is one of many academics, philosophers, and writers now commenting on a dramatic decline in the sense of community in America.

Because of our lack of genuine communities, work has become the place where many Americans attempt to satisfy yearnings for a sense of belonging. Our jobs are where we form our main niche communities. However, jobs are only places we visit from nine to five. We share employment, not our lives, with our workmates. Retirement, downsizing, and career changes bring us face-to-face with how transient our work relationships really are. We may make friends at work, but work does not offer the same sense of continuity, belonging, and profound connection that exists within genuine communities.

Ray Oldenburg contends that people need a "third place," outside of work and home, where they can connect with others.[7] If home is the first place, and work the second, then the informal meeting place in town, at a village green, or on a main street is the third. That "third place" is within walking distance of people's homes. It is where people gather on a consistent basis to share the process of living, where a sense of connection and belonging forms.

In England, the local pub or high street (what we would call main street) is that gathering place. In Italy, it is the piazzas and pedestrian streets dotted throughout their towns and cities. In France, it is the café. Every country except America has places where people can mingle, coexist, and establish bonds. The urban landscapes in other nations were specifically designed to have such locations.

America, on the other hand, since the end of World War II has not designed its physical landscape to accommodate the need for community, and now a sense of isolation is always close to the surface in the suburbs. This has had a profoundly negative impact on every American. In another of his books, *A Responsive Society*, Amitai Etzioni points out that sociology and psychology have shown that individuals are not able to function effectively without deep links to others in a community.[8] This does not mean that Americans cannot or do not find happiness or fulfillment. They can and do. However, it is primarily in narrow niche communities, and that fulfillment is less than it would be in genuine communities.

Sprawl is Expensive

Along with denying us the fulfillment of a robust community life, sprawl is also a heavy economic burden. By continuously developing land further and further out from already established civic infrastructure, sprawl increases local taxes, imposes significant national overhead costs, and is detrimentally expensive on a personal level as well.

How Sprawl Increases Local Taxes

The idea that new suburban developments strengthen the local tax base is a fantasy. Certainly, to local governments each new development means increased property, sales, and income taxes. However, what most local governments do not yet grasp is that this increased tax revenue is immediately offset by newly-required infrastructure services.

For each new suburban development, new water, sewage, utility, and road systems need to be built, and police, fire, and educational services must be provided. A study by American Farmland Trust shows that for every tax dollar collected from newly developed suburban residential property, about $1.25 in services must be paid for — a loss of 25 cents. In contrast, if agricultural farmland and open space are maintained, only 30 cents in services are spent for every tax dollar received — a gain of 70 cents.[9]

Education is the primary cost that local governments must absorb once sprawl comes along. As Jill Schwartz, American Farmland Trust's at-large field director, emphasizes: "We like to point out that cows don't go to school. Any increases in tax revenues that come from residential development are lost when you consider the cost of delivering necessary services."[10]

Former Maryland Governor Paris Glendening summed up some of the costs related to sprawl at his induction as president of the National Association of Governors in 1998 when he said, "Every new classroom costs $90,000. Every mile of new sewer line costs roughly $200,000. And every single-lane mile of new road costs at least four million dollars."

More significantly, the increased infrastructure costs associated with sprawl are not paid by those who create them. Real estate developers and homebuilders get a free ride. Instead, the burden is shifted to existing residents through higher local taxes. (See "Appendix B: Sprawl Raises Local Taxes" for examples of the hidden costs of sprawl from all over the country.)

Personally Expensive

Aside from taxes, sprawl is personally expensive in other ways. For example, over the span of 30 years — the same length as a basic home mortgage — an average American family will spend $560,000 on automobiles and have very little to show for that expenditure. This figure is based on a family owning two cars and trading them in every seven years. The cost breakdown is as follows. With an average car having a list price of $20,000, an average annual price inflation of 5 percent per car over 30 years, plus finance charges of 10 percent per car, we will spend $440,000 on cars during a 30-year period. Add to this the annual costs associated with regular maintenance, gas, and insurance, which comes to about $4,000 per year, or $120,000 over 30 years. Combine $120,000 with $440,000 and we will have spent over a half a million dollars in 30 years with very little to show for it except a gas-guzzler leaking oil in the driveway.[11]

Now, if we compare the average cost of commuting by public transportation to commuting by car, we would spend around $5 a day on mass transit. In a 200-workday year, that comes to only $1,000 a year. Over 30 years that is a mere $30,000 outlay. Multiply that by two people, and we will have spent only $60,000, compared to $560,000 for owning two cars.

If sprawl did not make us dependent on cars, we could conceivably save $500,000 over a 30-year period. Imagine what you could do with over half a million dollars. You could put your kids through college, buy that second home you've always wanted, or retire sooner.

National Overhead Costs

Aside from the individual costs associated with sprawl, our over-dependency on automobiles is also incredibly expensive on the national level. The United States needs more oil than any other country to keep its economy running. Per capita consumption of petroleum products is 459 gallons in the United States. The closest European nation is Germany, with only 140 gallons used per person each year.[12]

Some of that consumption is for industrial output, but the primary consumers of oil are American citizens. Because our urban landscape is such a sprawled mess, much of our oil consumption is through automobile usage. As sprawl forces every American to rely on a private car for transportation, we must import more oil per capita than any other nation.

The military costs of protecting the flow of oil from the Middle East have been immense, especially now that we are embroiled in the quagmire of a war in Iraq. For over 50 years the US has maintained a military presence with naval fleets, airfields, and other military installations and personnel in and around the Persian Gulf to ensure the safe passage of the American economy's lifeblood: oil. It is estimated that the tab for this US military presence, which is there solely to protect the supply of oil, currently costs between $30 and $60 billion annually.[13] The US government is also estimated to have spent between $61 and $71 billion during the Gulf War in the 1990s defending its oil interests.[14] It is safe to assume that the cost of our involvement in the Middle East is now much higher, considering that Congress recently passed a bill for $87 billion to help rebuild Iraq.

On the domestic front, we spend nearly $200 million a day constructing streets and roads. That adds up to $73 billion a year.

We spend $20 billion every year on routine road maintenance, such as clearing snow and filling potholes. Another $48 billion is spent annually on highway related services, including traffic and parking coordination and law enforcement, accident response teams, and the administration of federal, state, and city departments of transportation and motor vehicle bureaus. Every year a total of $6.3 billion goes to interest and debt retirement on highway bonds.[15]

Lost productivity and decreased economic vitality are other serious consequences of over-dependence on automobiles. The US General Accounting Office estimates national productivity losses caused by highway congestion at $100 billion a year. Air pollution from automobile emissions results in illness, hospitalization, and premature death calculated by the National Transportation Board to cost somewhere between $10 billion and $200 billion a year.[16]

The Urban Institute for the Federal Highway Administration (FHA) calculates the cost of all auto accidents at $358 billion annually, including 5,000,000 injuries a year — 1,800,000 of them disabling. In conjunction, nearly 45,000 people are killed *every year* in auto accidents. This is roughly equivalent to the total number of American deaths during the entire Vietnam War. The same study by the FHA quantifies the cost of pain, suffering, and reduced quality of life at $228 billion a year and estimates property damage at roughly $40 billion a year, mostly in wrecked vehicles.[17]

These numbers total more than $1 trillion dollars a year, all of which is passed on to US citizens through higher taxes. And all we get for this immense expenditure is that we are forced to own an automobile to get anywhere. This $1 trillion a year does not give Americans any of the alternatives to roads and highways that Europeans have, such as high-speed rail, extensive passenger rail, local and commuter rail, and intra-city trolleys.

The belief that suburban sprawl is an economic windfall for society and individuals is a myth we have been force-fed for decades. In reality, sprawl empties our souls through the isolation and alienation it creates, picks our pockets through increased taxation and automobile dependency, and is bankrupting the nation. Furthermore, as we will see later, sprawl puts every American at risk of violence.

Sprawl Was Not Preordained

In the annals of American history, there exists a myth that the marketplace determined the emergence of sprawl and automobile dominance. Americans are taught that where they live is a reflection of their individual choices, and the choices of Americans who came before them. They are led to believe that sprawl was inevitable, and that mass transit trolley systems and passenger railroads were a casualty of Adam Smith's invisible hand. Americans are told that their cities were abandoned because no one wanted to live in them anymore, and that the automobile reigns supreme because it was triumphant in a free and open competition for American consumers. This is, at best, a distortion of the truth.

Sprawl and America's dependency on the automobile were not preordained, and they certainly do not reflect an unbiased marketplace at work. A coordinated effort to alter the US urban landscape began during and immediately after World War II when corporate interests were permitted to illegally drive the extensive and beloved American trolley systems out of business. The most significant system that was unlawfully dismantled in this nationwide pattern of public transit destruction was in Los Angeles. It may be hard to picture, but LA, the current poster child for all that is wrong with an automobile-dependent society, once had the most extensive mass transportation system in the world.

The Pacific Electric Railway served the entire Los Angeles area — from the San Bernardino Valley in the east to Santa Monica's beaches, from San Fernando in the north to the oil fields at San Pedro — and contained 1,164 miles of inter- and intra-urban electric trolley track (see Figure 2.1).[18] More than 2,700 trains a day left from the center of LA to outlying stations like Redlands, Corona, Santa Monica, Redondo Beach, and Balboa.[19] It was the largest and most widely used public transportation system anywhere on the globe. However, as you have probably surmised, the scale of LA's public transit system did not stop its demise.

In 1943, when people desperately needed adequate and affordable transportation because of the shortages brought on by the war, the Los Angeles electric railroad and trolley system was purchased by the highway lobby — an illegal corporate cartel made up of automobile, oil, rubber, road construction, finance and bus companies — and unceremoniously put out of business. The tracks were immediately torn up and transmission lines ripped down, stranding the majority of the population who had depended on it for transport. Today, often on or next to these trolley routes, lines of cars sit caught in gridlock.

Regrettably, LA was not an isolated situation. During and immediately after World War II, the corporations of the highway lobby knowingly disregarded the Sherman Antitrust Laws by illegally destroying trolley companies all over the country. What this loss meant to Americans was that their suburbs would no longer have a focus; they would no longer be small towns built around public transport stops. Transit-oriented development became a thing of the past. The "highwaymen" completely altered America's urban landscape to fit their desire to profit from building more roads, selling more cars, and filling them with petroleum-based products. (To learn more about how the highway lobby illegally destroyed America's trolley systems, refer to "Appendix A: How Sprawl Came to Be.")

Our government was a willing conspirator in this plan to change America into an auto-dependent sprawled nation. This reality is illuminated by post-World War II era government transportation expenditures, where 75 percent of all money went towards the construction of roads, and only 1 percent went towards urban mass transit.[20] Little has changed today.

Figure 2.1

PACIFIC ELECTRIC RAILWAY IN LOS ANGELES, CALIFORNIA

Courtesy of the Orange Empire Railways Museum, Perris, California.

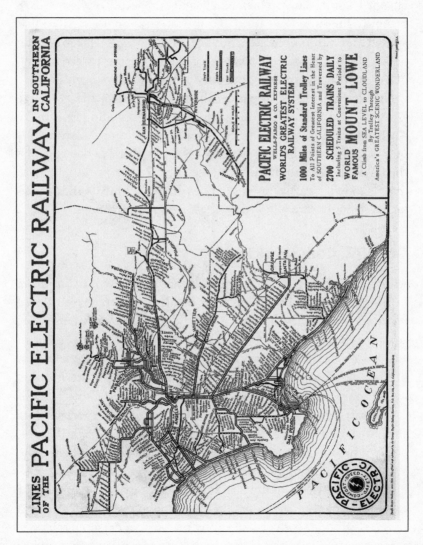

At one time, the LA trolley system was the world's largest. Overall, America's public transportation systems prior to World War II were the envy of other nations. Now they are a laughing stock.

Since 1945, our physical landscape has been molded by business interests, working hand in hand with government, to promote a sprawled way of life dominated by automobile usage. Tax laws were changed, zoning laws implemented, and our elected representatives blatantly supported one form of transport over another. All so that sprawl and automobile dependence would occur. The American people did not *choose* to live this way. On the contrary, since the end of World War II, sprawl is the only option we have been given.

In fact, as will be explained in more detail in the "Manage Growth" and "Change Zoning Laws" sections, zoning laws make it illegal to build anything but sprawl in America. Although it may seem hard to believe, since World War II it has been against the law to build community-oriented small towns complete with main streets, nearby homes, and schools within walking distance. What we are left with is the alienation of sprawl.

Genuine Communities

At this juncture, I should point out that the growth of suburbia in America has had some positive results. Suburbs have offered us increased privacy, less population density, and in many cases advantages in terms of education, employment and recreation. However, sprawl does not offer the most important element needed to keep a society safe and its people happy and fulfilled — genuine communities.

Genuine communities are made up of stores where residents shop, restaurants and cafés where neighbors and friends meet, parks where people gather, as well as offices, schools, public buildings, and a wide variety of housing options all within walking distance. The functions of life are laid out in a manner that accommodates and connects the people who use them.

Lively public spaces let a healthy network of personal relationships develop based on direct, face-to-face contact. In genuine communities, the shopkeepers, café owners, and restaurateurs are custodians of the public space, the maitre d's of the urban arena. They know you, you know them, and they help to connect you to the place and to others. Neighbors in a community are your support structure, your amicable acquaintances, people who make up a vast extended family of responsible adults.

These consistent interpersonal interactions that occur in genuine communities allow people to live together and share common goals despite having different interests and economic levels. Genuine communities are omnipresent yet invisible and offer a supportive structure of interdependent citizens who care for each other without being intrusive. Genuine communities are filled with intangible social assets that are intuitively understood and appreciated, such as mutual recognition, easy participation, and an identity rooted in a sense of place.

A sense of place is an important factor in the development and maintenance of community as it provides a physical location and spiritual focus for connection with others. People within a genuine community actively participate and cooperate with others, in formal and informal activities, to create their own sense of self-worth while also caring for others, which helps to develop a spirit of connectedness to the whole.[21]

Members of a genuine community possess a sense of trust, common purpose, mutual respect, and a bond with one another. This process of integration is, in a very real sense, how one's character is formed. By growing up in a communal environment, one learns about loyalty, commitment, and responsibility to something greater than oneself.[22]

One of the major benefits of a genuine community is that it contributes to the psychological health of its members. This well-being is created by the relationships that animate the community itself, associations that help people find meaning in their lives that transcends their individual existence. And when individuals, through this web of relationships, achieve a sense of fulfillment that includes others, a sense of community is created.[23]

In a genuine community you are never isolated; you need not be alone unless you choose to be. Just by walking out your door, you can be instantly transported into a world filled with companionship and human interaction. Communities are places that are designed to support and integrate our lives rather than fragment them, as is the case in sprawl.

If you grew up in a cohesive neighborhood or small town, perhaps this scenario, excerpted from Richard L. Curwin and Allen N. Mendler's book, *As Tough as Necessary,* sounds familiar to you: "When you walked to school each morning, you knew you would pass your friend's father waiting for the bus to go to work. Occasionally you would see another friend's mother peeking out of her window checking out the people in the street. Yet another mother would wave hello and tell you to have a nice day. These people knew you and you knew them. They made you feel protected and safe."[24]

This sense of community, of connectedness to others, once experienced — even if only as a temporary feeling during a crisis — is so compelling that the natural urge is to re-create and sustain it. Regrettably, here in the US, genuine communities have been relegated to the trash heap of history, remembered only through nostalgic movies such as "It's a Wonderful Life," the 1947 classic about small town life starring Jimmy Stewart. Having a sense of community is no longer a reality for most Americans. In fact, the opposite is generally true. This situation has contributed to an over-reliance on the artificial reality of television, a medium that offers only a flickering substitute for community life.

TV as Artificial Community

As a result of the alienation of sprawl, American "communities" now come prepackaged, ready to enjoy, beamed at us from our television sets. Many Americans now value their television viewing more than interpersonal activity, or at least treat it with the same significance. TV has become such a staple of our existence, and such a powerful influence in our lives, that instead of developing relationships with real companions, many Americans seem more concerned with fictional television characters.

This unhealthy attachment became evident when the long-running soap opera "Another World" went off the air in 1999. Fans went into mourning. They gathered in bars and restaurants to watch the last episode together. Viewers described the characters in the show as family, and compared the show's demise to that of a friend dying. People had spent decades of their lives with these characters and felt a profound sense of loss when the show ended.[25] This bizarre connection to fictional characters is not considered abnormal here in America. In the absence of genuine communities, television has taken on an absurdly prominent role in our society.

Dr. John Maltby, of the University of Leicester in England, has even reported a new mental disorder, called Celebrity Worship Syndrome, in the *Journal of Nervous and Mental Disease.* Dr. Maltby claims that for some people, the media is not just entertainment, but has "a clinical component." He postulates that this is likely due to the dominance of TV and the breakdown of family and community. Because of this, individuals are replacing the real companions in their lives with celebrities.[26]

With cable and satellite TV spanning the globe, television is as available in other countries as it is in the US. Even so, television simply does not play as significant a role in everyday life elsewhere as it does in America. Statistics show that most Americans watch 23 percent more television than their counterparts in Western Europe.[27]

One possible reason for this is that these countries offer their citizens a more interesting, rewarding, and fulfilling alternative to electronic entertainment — genuine communities. In other nations, there are still livable and safe places to walk, where people can stop for dinner, dessert, or a drink, and meet neighbors and friends. Consequently, TV viewing is not as prevalent. Real life, when available, will always win out over fantasy.

One excellent example of this is a small town in the United Kingdom called Waddington. In this town, as shown by an overall dearth of subscriptions to cable TV, there was clear lack of interest in that entertainment option. Feeling challenged to change the town's TV viewing habits, the British media began offering free programming to the citizens of Waddington. They could watch porn channels, sports, gardening shows and more, all on a free trial basis for three months. After the trial was over, and the people of Waddington were offered the opportunity to sign up for the service, not a single viewer wanted to continue access. Television simply could not compete with the vibrancy of Waddington's community.[28] Even though television viewing has been woven into the fabric of everyday life all over Europe, community life stills reigns supreme.

Communities Exist Outside America

Societies outside the United States understand what renowned psychologist Thomas Moore asserts in his book *Care of the Soul*: "One of the strongest needs of the soul is for community."[29] As a result of this understanding, European cities and their suburbs are quite different from their counterparts in America. Suburban sprawl simply does not exist in Europe to the extent it does here. Nor have Europeans allowed their inner cities to be turned into highways, office ghettos, and parking garages. As a result, genuine communities continue to thrive everywhere in Europe.

European cities have always included public spaces where people can connect with others. In fact, their cities and towns were designed specifically to bring people together. In Italy, for example, when cities were laid out centuries ago, each neighborhood was given its own piazza so that people had a place to gather. Today, to counterbalance the impact of the automobile, entire sections of most European cities have been turned into pedestrian zones allowing communities to continue to blossom and grow. Within European cities and towns, a sense of belonging and community thrives. In such places, according to Mary Hommann, an authority on urban planning, "People live close together in dignity; and give attention and service to each other with cordiality."[30]

Europeans have not been afraid to plan, and using knowledge learned from centuries of urban development they have done so in a coherent manner. Europe has a long history of regulating and subordinating selfish private interests for the welfare of the entire society. In 1946, England passed the New Towns Act, which to date has seen the construction of over 50 new towns complete with all the functions of life.

While America pursued the path of sprawl, the British were easing the population pressure in their cities by creating vibrant small and medium sized towns all connected by extensive public transit. This is not to say that Britain does not have its share of unsightly billboards, leveled landmarks, and other forms of "progress"; but it is in far better control of its natural and built environment than the United States.[31]

Another modern example of how Europeans have managed their urban spaces is through their restrictions on the use of utilities in undeveloped areas. Gas, sewage, and water lines are not permitted in many locales without considerable thought and study. A case in point is a law passed in Italy in 1967 which decreed that real estate speculators would have to pay the costs of "primary urbanization" (such as roads, electricity, gas, etc.) and part of the costs of "secondary urbanization," which includes schools, parks, and other necessary urban amenities.[32] This helped to curb the spread of unplanned sprawl, allowed for more intelligent planning, and helped to preserve the beauty and livability of Italian towns, cities, and rural expanses. Imagine if we did that here, in the US.

European cities and towns are amazing places to live in or visit, despite the fact that many of these urban centers were completely destroyed by bombing during World War II. After that overwhelming destruction, European cities were laboriously rebuilt to become places where people and communities could once again thrive. In the same time period, on the other hand, American cities and towns, untouched by those two world conflagrations, were demolished by government-sponsored highway construction and unproven "urban renewal" projects. Indeed, if one were not familiar with the two world wars, whose major battles were fought in Europe, one might conclude that it was American cities that were bombed, judging from their abandoned and decaying buildings and rubble-strewn vacant lots.

For centuries Europeans have been planning intelligently, under the auspices and guidance of national and local governments, to make their urban spaces livable. The result is that European cities and towns are built and maintained to accommodate the needs of the people. Even our closest neighbor, Canada, has followed a more European path of urban development.

Though they have made similar mistakes in the urban arena, Canada seems to have learned more quickly from them and implemented improvements faster. For example, Canada initially jumped on the American-inspired bandwagon of urban renewal by implementing laws to raze slums. However, while American cities continue to level entire city blocks today, four decades ago, in 1964, Canadian urban renewal was changed to focus on rehabilitation rather than razing of substandard housing.

In conjunction, Canada initially began to implement unrestrained suburban sprawl along with the US. However, when introduced to the concept of building suburban towns rather than sprawl, Canada embraced this option instead. One example is the locality of Don Mills in the greater Toronto area. Built from 1952–62 on 800 hectares with a community shopping centre and high school at the intersection of two roads and four neighborhoods, it has the makings of a small town. Don Mills was the trendsetter that established the subsequent pattern of Canadian urban expansion creating small towns and complete neighborhoods.

Another aspect that sets Canada apart from the U.S. is that urban and transportation planning occurs nationally and regionally as well as locally. One example is when the province of Ontario revised its planning act in 1946 to include all the cities, towns, and townships within its borders. No state in the US has anything resembling such planning authority.

Though not perfect in their implementation of urban revitalization or suburban development, Canada's approach has been more sustainable and more community-oriented than that of their neighbors to the south. Canada still has its share of problems. It needs more transportation options, updated infrastructure, a wider choice of housing, better environmental solutions, and more investment in city centers. But overall, Canada continues to do a much better job of maintaining the integrity of its urban spaces than the United States. As a result, Toronto, Montreal, Quebec, and Vancouver are some of the most livable cities on this continent.[33]

American cities and suburbs, on the other hand, have been haphazardly thrown together, the product of continued collusion between developers and local governments to enhance real-estate profits and build more efficient arteries for automobile traffic. As a result, most Americans can no longer recall what life was like before suburbia, our massive highway system, and the urban blight they've both created.

We used to have beautiful old buildings in all our cities, magnificent stone and brick structures, intricately decorated, aesthetically appealing, and surrounded by vibrant, safe, and livable neighborhood communities. Many of our urban areas were reminiscent of the great cities of Europe. A prime example is Washington, DC, designed by the French urban planner Pierre L'Enfant and modeled after Paris, France. The majority of the buildings in downtown DC used to be architectural wonders, and old photos of that city clearly show its European heritage. Now, however, the center of DC is a bland glass, steel, and concrete office park, and many other parts of the city are filled with empty lots and the shells of abandoned buildings. This situation is the same in every American city. Instead of respecting, cherishing, and maintaining our older buildings, we tear them down. (For more information on the history of sprawl, see "Appendix A: How Sprawl Came to Be".)

Why do so many Americans flock to European cities and towns on their vacations? Deep in our souls, we long for the livability of these well-preserved urban cores. We crave the community they nurture, so we travel to Europe to find it.

Outside of America, gatherings in genuine communities are the norm. People meet informally at all times of the day. The men may congregate together, as do the women, and the children usually find their own spot, but interaction among the groups is common. Watching these informal gatherings is like witnessing a complex social interplay of contented citizens.

These people may have little in common with each other except that they live in the same town or city neighborhood. They have different jobs, dissimilar income and housing levels, and unique personal interests; they belong to a variety of clubs; their children go to different schools. However, in these communities, possibly because of everyone's dissimilarity, people tend to savor the common bonds of community they share.

People in other countries have their families and friends, as well as groups that they belong to. However, their daily bond with an extended community of diverse people helps to make life more robust and balanced than what we experience in America.

Even Australia, a country very much like ours in terms of its age and size, has not allowed its communities or physical landscape to be destroyed the way America has. Bill Bryson, a best-selling author who has spent over two decades outside of America, notes in his critically acclaimed book, *The Lost Continent: Travels in Small Town America,* all the amenities that have disappeared in America in the last two decades because of sprawl. "I've spent a lot of time in Australia this last year," he writes, "and the thing that's amazing to me is how much it was like America in the 1950s. It rammed it home to me how much we've lost. They still have coherent small towns with vibrant Main Streets."[34]

Here in America we may have acquired variety and convenience, but we've given up community. As Bryson says, "It's very hard to argue that going shopping at the mall or Wal-Mart or a fast-food place aren't easy and convenient and save you time, but it's hard to argue that any of them is a quality experience."[35] The concept of what constitutes quality of life in the US has been transformed over the years into something commercial rather than social. We have a vast array of products to choose from, all at rock bottom prices, and we have been told that this enhances our quality of life. However, if we peel back the façade of this cultural paradigm, we quickly realize that consumer products don't cause our souls to sing or make us feel loved. Inexpensive products don't give us a sense of belonging or a connection to others the way being part of a community would. But in the empty expanses of sprawl, this is all we have. In suburbia, our lives have been reduced to a series of commercial transactions that are devoid of community interaction. The way America has separated the functions of life has not only changed the landscape, but has had a dramatically negative impact on most Americans' quality of life as well.

Change is in the Air

Every year, more and more Americans are beginning to recognize that sprawl is not such a great place to live after all. This realization has fostered the emergence of an architectural and development movement called New Urbanism that began in the mid-1980s as a way to sway developers from building car-dependent subdivisions, and inspire them to create people-friendly narrow streets, houses with front porches, multi-use buildings, and a variety of homes in each development for every income level. Though it has its detractors, New Urbanism is the vanguard in helping to recreate genuine communities in America.

New Urbanism

A prime example of New Urbanism is Disney's successful development in Celebration, Florida. This 5,000-acre patch of Florida shrub next to the Magic Kingdom has been converted into a small town that includes all the elements needed for a vibrant community. Celebration is one of the most watched of the neo-traditional towns springing up across the United States, and will be home to 20,000 residents when completed. With a central core containing shops, cafés, restaurants, offices, and apartments above the stores, Celebration is truly a return to small-town living. Radiating from this central core are different economic levels of housing, with the least expensive and smaller residences situated closer to the core.

Residents in Celebration can walk downtown, greeting neighbors along the way. Children can play outside under the watchful eye of other adult members of the community. Parents can feel confident knowing their children are usually just minutes from home — walking distance — in the center of town or at a nearby playground or park. In Celebration, parents understand the value of having their children socialize in an environment that is more wholesome than the consumer-oriented environment of a shopping mall. And they especially appreciate the centralized, pedestrian-friendly design because it means they don't have to drive their kids everywhere.

People in Celebration have returned to the way life used to be before sprawl destroyed our country. Residents talk about their sense of community, their friendly and caring neighbors, and about how the school and attractive town center are easily accessible. Moreover, the proximity of the houses has led to what some Celebration residents refer to as their "porch culture," where people actually sit on their porches and socialize with passersby.[36] All these aspects of their town give each resident a degree of independence, as well as social connections, which would not exist if they lived in sprawl.

New Urbanism developments such as Celebration are not perfect, mainly because they are privately managed and controlled. This privatization of public life has the potential to reduce diversity, increase segregation, and lead to exclusion rather than express the embrace of genuine communities. Another drawback is that in most cases these developments are in new locations instead of existing urban environments. This continues the costly pattern of abandoning existing infrastructure. An additional flaw is that these new developments are not linked by viable public transport. This maintains an unhealthy dependence on the automobile, which tends to isolate people from one another, and can reduce community interaction.

Yet another defect with some New Urbanism developments is that they are architectural showcases rather than places where true community can form. To save on costs or to avoid having to get zoning laws changed, some New Urbanism developments do not have the main streets necessary to encourage people to walk around and mingle. The houses may have front porches, but if no one is walking, porches have little impact on social interaction. As professor John Freie describes in his book, *Counterfeit Community*, these places are marketed as "communities," tugging at our longing to belong, our ache to connect to others, but they fulfill few of the needs for genuine community.

Though some New Urbanism developments are counterfeits of what is needed, they are still a step in the right direction. They are a clear indication that Americans are beginning to reject the anonymity of sprawl and are actively seeking community.

Whether it is called New Urbanism, Garden City Development, Transit Oriented Development, Traditional Neighborhood Development, or Smart Growth, projects are underway all over America that are beginning to do something about the fundamentally flawed urban landscape of sprawl. According to the *New Urban News* of Ithaca, New York, a newsletter that tracks the return to traditional neighborhood patterns, 648 new urbanism communities have been built, are under construction, or are in the planning stages.[37]

Fake Small Towns

A much more prevalent trend is the creation of places which I call "fake small towns." These illusions of livability are popping up all over the country, and are evident in Myrtle Beach, South

Carolina; San Diego, California; Tucson, Arizona; Reston, Virginia; and many places in between. These locations have well-planned townscapes with a "main street" look and feel, complete with quaint shops, bars, and restaurants, all linked by pedestrian-friendly sidewalks.

However, these aesthetically appealing townscapes are not real: no one lives in them. There are no homes, no permanent residents. No one goes to school or church there. No one grows old or raises children in these places. Though they have the look and feel of small towns, in reality they are just like sprawl. The people who frequent them are mainly strangers. There is no sense of genuine community. These places are much like an amusement park ride, "Small-Town Land," where people come, have dinner, spend some money, then leave.

These "fake small towns" are really only shopping malls turned inside out with some appealing architectural amenities added on. In fact, the name real estate developers give these places — "lifestyle centers" — clearly indicates the commercial rather than communitarian purpose.

Despite their limitations, a Virginia resident describes these places well when she says, "Reston Town Center may be fake, but it feels real. It is the only town we have. It is the only place we can go where we can see a movie, then walk to a restaurant, and afterwards sit in a park, or grab an ice cream."

The popularity of places like Reston Town Center clearly indicates that Americans crave a connection to community. Though flawed, these places are helping to introduce sprawl denizens to what communities can be like, and can help steer people back down the path of community livability that was abandoned over 50 years ago when sprawl enveloped the landscape.

Converted Shopping Malls
Another development trend, one which goes beyond building fake small towns, is converting abandoned or under-performing shopping malls into villages, complete with all the functions of

life including housing. These places are old-fashioned style small towns, where people live, work, and play within walking distance. With pedestrian friendly streets, sidewalks, and storefronts filled with cafés, restaurants, and shops, old shopping malls are being turned into places where new communities are forming. Examples can be found in Winter Park, Florida; St. Paul, Minnesota; and Lakewood, Colorado. There are a number in various stages of development in Orange County, California.[38] The re-purposing of these old malls into new villages is the clearest indicator to me that America is finally waking up from the nightmare of sprawl. If we build on the momentum from these existing projects, it is quite possible that the next generation of Americans will have the opportunity to savor the safety and sense of belonging associated with living in genuine communities.

PART ONE

Sprawl's Human Impact

"For the past fifty years, we Americans have been building a national landscape that is largely devoid of places worth caring about. Soulless subdivisions, residential 'communities' utterly lacking in communal life; strip shopping centers, 'big box' chain stores, and artificially festive malls set within barren seas of parking; antiseptic office parks, ghost towns after 6 PM; and mile upon mile of clogged collector roads."

— Andres Duany, Elizabeth Plater-Zyberk, Jeff Speck, *Suburban Nation: The Rise of Sprawl and the Decline of the American Dream*

"For 93 percent of all trips outside the home, for whatever distance and whatever purpose, Americans now get in a car. On average the total walking of an American these days — that's walking of all types: from the car to office, from office to car, around the supermarket and shopping malls — adds up to 1.4 miles a week, barely 350 yards a day. No wonder studies have shown that sprawl is linked to obesity."

— Bill Bryson, *A Walk in the Woods*

CHAPTER TWO

A Society of Strangers

Anyone having dual familiarity with prewar small
towns and modern shopping malls will be repelled
by the comparison. Totally unlike Main Street the
shopping mall is populated by strangers.

— Ray Oldenburg

BY ITS VERY NATURE, SPRAWL ISOLATES AMERICANS from one
another. The zoned segregation of sprawl has dramatically
separated the functions of daily life so that even though
we are constantly surrounded by swarms of people, the vast
majority of them are strangers. Outside of work and other structured activities, we go through our days without being recognized by others. We can spend our waking hours running
errands, going to the gym, shopping for clothes, having lunch at
a bistro, going to a movie, and not encounter a soul we know.
These days of anonymity can turn into weeks, the weeks into
months, the months into years, and the years into a lifetime. This
is what it is like to live in sprawl; it is the antithesis of community. The suburban experience simply does not include
interaction with people embedded in a common social network.

We go through life in the presence of others, but not in their company.

We all have friends, but these people typically do not live nearby. Our family members, too, even if they live in the same metropolitan area, usually reside in a distant subdivision that typically reflects their earning power rather than any connection they may have to the place. Aside from our immediate nuclear family, those significant to us do not generally play an active role in our everyday lives. Instead, we spend our time among strangers when out in public, or with acquaintances at work.

Our time at home is no longer spent outdoors among our neighbors, who once would have made up our community. Without the central cores of small towns, Americans do not have the opportunity to gather in places where they are recognized, such as a local bookstore, café, restaurant, library, or the town square. The end result is that we now interact more with technology than with real people. We spend more time laughing at TV jokes than with each other. We spend more time watching fictional "friends" on TV than we do getting together with our real friends. We spend more time on the phone or in Internet chat rooms than talking to people face-to-face. Without small town main streets and the like offering Americans easy, informal places to gather, we have become a nation of isolated individuals, a society of strangers.

This anonymity is hazardous to our mental health. Being recognized is powerfully therapeutic. Each of us has experienced being somewhere on our own — whether it is the mall, shopping center, or city street — and then running into someone we know. Suddenly, we are no longer alone. We are recognized. In other countries, that experience happens regularly. In the sprawled expanses of suburbia it happens rarely. Without such serendipitous interactions, life can seem less than fulfilling.

Communities provide us with a context for our lives, helping us feel a part of something other than ourselves. Communities give us an identity rooted in sense of place, allowing us to feel that we belong, that we have value. Through these social relationships and responsibilities our lives touch and are touched by others, fostering a greater compassion and awareness for the needs of those around us. Without this web of connectivity found in genuine communities, American life has become isolating and alienating.

At the same time, we all need privacy at some time or another. Solitude speaks to the part of us that yearns to break free from the thoughts and expectations of others. However, the all-pervasive sense of isolation that exists in America is excessive and unhealthy. In the following sections you will see how the anonymous nature of American life crushes our spirit by increasing loneliness and depression, steals quality time from our lives, segregates the elderly from the rest of society, and negatively impacts the healthy development of our children.

Loneliness and Depression

Environmental psychologists have found that people who are integrated into a local community network report fewer symptoms of psychological disturbances than individuals who are socially isolated.[1] Doctors warn that isolation and alienation are risk factors for disease, much like smoking or drinking. Not only does the experience of being loved, cherished, and cared for protect people from disease, it also makes them feel as if life is worthwhile.[2]

Regrettably, in America today loneliness is rampant. Though we sometimes think of loneliness as an affliction of the elderly, isolated in their empty houses or in sterile nursing homes, studies indicate that all Americans are equally susceptible to the burden of loneliness. In one major survey, a quarter of US adults reported that they had felt extremely lonely at least once in the previous two weeks.[3]

Harvard political scientist Robert Putnam, in his book *Bowling Alone,* reports a rise in malaise and unhappiness among all Americans. Laura Pappalo in *The Connection Gap: Why Americans Feel So Alone,* writes about the epidemic of loneliness in this country. In *The Ambitious Generation,* sociologists Barbara Schneider and David Stevenson show that American teenagers are now spending more time alone than they ever have before — three and a half hours each day. American children spend more time alone than with family or friends. These findings are supported by Mary Eberstadt's book, *Home-Alone America,* which goes on to say that isolation is the root cause of most of the ills that beset American youngsters. Finally, a study by psychologist Nicholas Zill finds that 10 percent of children between the ages of 12 and 16 consider themselves to be frequently lonely. As these studies and books indicate, Americans are experiencing a scourge of isolation and deep felt sense of alienation.[4]

Significantly, loneliness has been identified as a major cause of the intense emotional pain that can lead to despair, thoughts of suicide, and an increased incidence of other psychological problems.[5] Dr. Edward Shorter, Ph.D., a medical historian on the faculty of Medicine at the University of Toronto, has found that Americans today have more medical complaints than they did a few decades ago, especially ones that doctors consider to be psychological in nature.[6] Backing up this assessment is a more recent government-sponsored study featured in the June 2005 issue of the *Archives of General Psychiatry*, which indicates that "one quarter of all Americans met the criteria for having a mental illness within the past year."[7] The study goes on to suggest that the reason for the lower levels of mental health problems among minorities could be the social support that exists within these populations.

Another survey, this one a compilation of nearly 300 studies, found that typical schoolchildren and college students in the 1980s reported more anxiety than did child psychiatric patients in the 1950s. As social support and connection have significantly decreased because of sprawl, anxiety and other expressions of personal angst have measurably increased.[8] The American Medical Association has determined that the number of people being treated for depression has increased dramatically in the United

States, more than tripling between 1987 and 1997.[9] According to the National Institute of Mental Health, ten percent of Americans suffer from depression in any given year.[10] That's almost 30 million people!

This sense of despair has contributed to the increase in suicides in America, especially among the young. Americans from 15 to 19 years old were four times as likely to kill themselves in 1988 as in 1950.[11] Today, suicide is the third leading cause of death among teenagers aged 15 to 19 — after motor vehicle accidents and unintentional injury.[12] Suicides kill over 30,000 Americans each year; for every two people murdered, there are three who commit suicide. What is even more frightening is that more than eight million Americans have contemplated suicide, and more than six million have had continuous thoughts about ending their lives. [13]

As all of these statistics and studies indicate, loneliness and depression are serious problems in America. Even people who do not consider themselves unhappy or lonely tend to exhibit classic behaviors associated with these problems. Americans over-eat, over-spend, over-entertain, and over-medicate themselves to compensate for the emptiness of their lives. People watch too much TV, buy too much stuff, play too many video games, and watch too many movies in an attempt to fill the void left by a lack of community. Americans spend their money and their time trying to find fulfillment without realizing that it is their urban landscape that denies them much of what they seek.

Isolation of the Elderly

Senior citizens are particularly vulnerable to the adverse effects of sprawl. Because there are no genuine communities in sprawl, an increasing number of seniors are being isolated from life, trapped in their suburban homes with few people to interact with. This situation is especially true if a person can no longer drive. With no convenient places to walk in sprawl, seniors instantly lose out on the life-sustaining, soul-enriching experience of informal human contact.

This reduced interaction is resulting in an epidemic of depression among America's elderly. According to the National Institute of Mental Health, among the 35 million Americans over the age of 65, 2 million suffer from a clinical form of depression, and another 5 million report symptoms associated with depression.[14]

Dr. John Siberski, director of geriatric psychiatry at Georgetown University Hospital in Washington, DC, asserts that social support is the key to preventing many forms of depression.[15] Understanding this need for social interaction, many seniors move into retirement "communities" to maintain at least a semblance of connection to others. However, these places end up isolating seniors from other age groups as well as from the activities of real life. This can end up marginalizing their existence, making them feel less than useful, and lowering their self-esteem — all of which can also cause powerful feelings of depression and loneliness. Even though these retirement homes do supply a sense of connection as a result of shared meals and activities, they do not offer the same sense of belonging and full range of human experiences as genuine communities.

The healthy sense of belonging that comes from being part of a genuine community is a matter of life and death for seniors. Study after study has shown that emotional well-being is a key factor to living a healthy and long life, especially as one gets older. Besides increasing physical health, involvement with friends, family, and community can fill seniors' lives with joy, purpose, and meaning, keeping them mentally and spiritually healthy as well.[16]

Sprawl's segregated environment disrupts an older person's circle of friends, shreds the cross-generational fabric of society, and prevents the passing on of wisdom, insight, knowledge, and experience. Sprawl creates an artificial schism between generations by first isolating seniors in their suburban homes then segregating them in retirement ghettoes.

The last years of our lives should be spent surrounded by our friends, family, and extended community, not shut in sterile retirement homes with only memories for companions. In sprawl we can no longer grow old with dignity, while remaining valued members of an extended community. Sprawl alienates and isolates every American, greatly reducing our chances of living full and rewarding lives all the way to the end. Unfortunately, only when age has diminished our mobility, do we finally realize how trapped we are in sprawl. But by then, it's too late.

Stolen Life

It's not just seniors who are marginalized in sprawl. Everyone's quality of life is reduced because the landscape of suburbia forces us to drive everywhere. All over America, driving times are increasing, road congestion is getting worse, and our lives suffer as a result. Cars may have initially made living easier, but that is no longer the case. They now make our lives miserable.

Our automobiles have become prisons, and the sentences we serve in them keep getting longer and longer — with no chance of parole unless drastic changes are made throughout our entire society. Because sprawl has so dramatically fragmented the functions of life, two and a half generations of Americans have missed out on the possibility of overall fulfillment that life has to offer, simply because we spend so much time trapped in our cars. It is extremely difficult to have meaningful interactions with other members of society from the confines of an automobile.

According to *State of the Cities Report 1999* prepared by the US Department of Transportation, the average American household drove 40 percent more in 1999 than in 1970. A Department of Housing and Urban Development study estimates that Americans spend over two hours each day in their cars. Endgridlock.org reports that we lose on average the equivalent of 31 days to commuting each year. Studies by the Sierra Club indicate that commuting times have increased twofold com-pared to ten years ago. And commuting distances are increasing as well. Between 1983 and 1995, the average round-trip commute to work in the United States grew 37 percent, to nearly 12 miles.[17]

The statistics may vary, but the reality is that without managed growth or viable transportation options other than the automobile, Americans are forced to spend more and more time in their cars. With no overall urban and transportation plan, houses continue to be built farther and farther away from urban centers, and the functions of life continue to be zoned apart, reducing public transportation's effectiveness while perpetuating our overdependence on automobiles.

Trapped in traffic, we have less time for civic engagements, pursuing hobbies, playing sports, taking walks, and spending time with friends or family. Our interpersonal relationships have been relegated to rushed phone conversations and quick e-mail messages. A key indicator of the personal isolation Americans feel is our increasing dependence on communications technology, which is expanding in direct proportion to the reduction in meaningful interpersonal interaction. We carry our BlackBerrys, cell phones, and laptops as badges of multitasking honor. We bristle with bandwidth and satellite access — online, hooked up, and cyber-savvy. But we still don't know our neighbors, and we don't have time for our friends.

It seems to me that cell phones have become so popular so quickly because they allow people to use the dead time in their cars to talk to their friends, whom they rarely see anymore. However, cell phone conversations, no matter how frequent, can never replace personal interaction. Technology will never fill the void that sprawl has created in our lives.

If we had livable communities in America, people would be able to meet face-to-face rather than bumper-to-bumper in traffic, or byte-to-byte on their cell phones. If our physical landscape had been planned properly, we could spend quality time with friends and family instead of being trapped behind the wheels of our automobiles, or isolated in our suburban homes.

Children's Stunted Development

One of the most dramatic human costs of sprawl is that American children are trapped in their suburban subdivisions, unable to get anywhere without parental assistance. Urban social scientist and successful author Philip Langdon, in his groundbreaking book *A Better Place to Live*, puts it clearly when he says: "Parents have ensconced their children in strictly residential subdivisions — removed from stores, offices, workplaces — on the assumption that this will make the children's lives safe. It may — for a while — but at the cost of impeding children's education, maturity, and independence."[18] Sprawl, to put it bluntly, is stunting the development of America's children.

Instead of getting to plan their own time, children in sprawl are squeezed into the schedules of already overextended parents who chauffeur them back and forth to organized activities, lessons, sports matches, and tutoring sessions. The spontaneity of play, the natural socialization of engaging with others, and the random exploration of one's surroundings are critical childhood learning experiences. As Dorothy Rich, founder and president of the Home and School Institute, emphasizes, "To grow up strong and confident, independent and dependable, all children need to be able to play spontaneously."[19] Yet in sprawl children's ability to move about freely has been all but eliminated. By confining children in isolated subdivisions, sprawl stifles the process by which they can develop into well-adjusted adults.

Children's recreation has ramifications for how they will experience and understand themselves. It also helps shape their attitudes and behavior towards others. The overstructured existence that sprawl has created hinders the ability of American children to develop into independent, free-thinking, creative human beings.

As sociologist Desmond Morris points out in his book, *The Naked Ape*, individuals raised in overly structured environments will find healthy relationships difficult to initiate or sustain. He then stresses that if such individuals do manage to become parents, they are more likely to be bad ones. If children do not experience the interaction of informal juvenile recreation groups and instead are always restricted in their play, they are more likely to become socially stunted adults.[20]

This assertion is not meant to imply that every American since the advent of sprawl is socially dysfunctional and incapable of raising healthy children. It simply states the obvious: when children are overscheduled and oversupervised, some of them lose coping skills and have more difficulty learning how to be independent, free-thinking adults. Unfortunately, that is how we are raising our kids in sprawl, and have been for decades. Growing up in such an environment can and does have a detrimental impact on people's social development.

Constant adult attention is also creating a lack of initiative in children. They don't understand that they have to work to accomplish things, that they have to sacrifice to achieve. If children do not learn early how to perform tasks on their own, without supervision, without guidance, they will be destined for increasingly dependent and unfulfilling lives. One manifestation of this type of upbringing is that when the going gets tough, these people point fingers instead of taking responsibility for their actions or finding a solution to their problems. They learn to blame other people and circumstances for their failures, because they've never learned that they are the ones who are ultimately responsible for themselves and their behavior.

Another manifestation of the growing attitude problem among children of sprawl is that college students are arriving unprepared for the rigors of higher education. Incoming college students today seem to have little desire to learn, to know and understand things outside their own narrow concerns. Students are "inattentive, easily bored, and unwilling to work hard, especially on difficult or abstract material outside their interests," according to a report in *The Washington Post*.[21] These spoon-fed future "leaders" of our country, on their way to becoming adults, are not prepared to take on that mantle of responsibility.

Things were not always this way. Sixty years ago, before sprawl, kids explored life in safe and vibrant communities. Today, American youth have far fewer opportunities for independent, personal growth. Without self-mobility, children are shackled to their parents for transportation or trapped at home, glued to the television or a computer game.

Parents in sprawl have limited opportunities to guide their children through the many stages of human development in a healthy and meaningful way. Because there are no corner stores and the supermarket is miles away, parents cannot send their children out for a loaf of bread to teach them about money and responsibility. Since a car is usually required to get anywhere, parents must do all the errands themselves, and their children miss out on the day-to-day life lessons that would help them develop into responsible, independent adults.

Even the manner in which American children get to school is overly structured. Because schools are segregated from the other functions of life, instead of being able to make their way independently, whether on foot, bicycle, or via public transportation, the majority of American children have to take school buses. At first glance, something as innocuous as taking a school bus does not seem detrimental to a child's development.

Viewed from another angle, however, the world, quite literally, comes to a stop for American children on their way to school. Parents take time out of their day to shepherd children to the bus stop and watch over them like hawks until the bus arrives. Traffic is then halted in both directions as the children board and the bus will not move until every child is seated. This situation, repeated every school day for nearly every child in America, unconsciously programs them to feel privileged, as if the world rotates around them.

Today in the US children rarely have to plan anything for themselves, manage their time, tally their resources, or begin the process of learning how to be independent, free-thinking individuals. As a result, many young people never learn how. American children have become passive observers, not active participants in life.

One possible consequence of this acquiescence is that once the children of sprawl become adults, they tend not to participate in the democratic process. If voter turnout is an indicator of people's ability and desire to manage their lives instead of having it managed for them, what we may be seeing with the low voter turnout in the US as compared to other developed nations is that American adults, the vast majority of whom have been raised in suburbia, are fulfilling the acquiescent destiny that sprawl has imprinted upon them. This situation is supported by statistics compiled by the Institute for Democracy and Electoral Assistance: the average percentage of the population voting in Congressional elections in the US from 1990 to 2000 was a mere 43.47 percent. Presidential elections averaged 50.55 percent over the same time period. Comparatively, in the United Kingdom, the European nation with the lowest voter turnout, the average was 65.77 percent, and in Germany it was 73.60 percent.[22]

Certainly, there are other forces at play limiting voter participation, such as absurdly shaped gerrymandered districts and the dominant influence of moneyed special interests. Sprawl, however, by stunting the independent, creative development of those raised in its environs, has also contributed to a decrease in civic participation, which in turn has a profoundly negative influence on the proper functioning of America's democracy.

Senator Hillary Rodham Clinton made famous the African proverb that legislators and teachers now like to repeat: "It takes a village to raise a child." However, sprawl has eliminated villages from America, and along with them went safe, healthy communities where our children can grow into well-adjusted individuals. Gina Adams, a researcher with the Urban Institute, explains that at one time "working parents could ... count on a neighborhood of caring, watchful adults to fill in the gap. [Now] neighborhoods are ghost towns during the day, regardless of economic background."[23] The environment of sprawl does little to help initiate

American children into becoming healthy and socially responsible adults.

For the past 50-plus years we've mistakenly believed that the suburbs are the best place to raise a family. However, author Ferenc Maté has it right when he says that our suburbs "do nothing to satisfy our social human needs; they do nothing to encourage us to be anything but strangers who happen to park their cars on the same street every night."[24] Though the suburbs seem like healthy places, everyone's quality of life is dramatically reduced in the society of strangers created by sprawl.

CHAPTER THREE

A Culture of Incivility

There is no higher religion than human service.
To work for the common good is the greatest creed.
— Albert Schweitzer

The physical landscape in which people live is well known to have a dramatic impact on society and the individuals in it. Environmental psychology deals specifically with how the built environment impacts human development, mental health, and behavior. A related field called psychogeography looks into how geographical settings affect the mood and behavior of individuals. There is a consensus in both of these disciplines that where we live clearly influences who we are and how we behave towards others.

Here in America, as over 70 percent of citizens now reside in the community-less expanses of sprawl, there are few opportunities for healthy and respectful social interactions. Without this foundation of community, many of us have not developed a sense of loyalty to others, a sense of belonging to a group, or the skills necessary to interact with strangers in public. Instead, we are being programmed to respond to situations in a manner that even in the very recent past would have been considered blatantly discourteous. Because of the sprawl-induced lack of genuine communities, the culture of American society has become rude and uncivil. We have lost the skills necessary to be a part of a civil society, skills that can be learned only by living in and learning from a community.

Any sociologist will tell you that individuals intuitively learn human relationship skills through observation and unconscious mimicry. Human beings are imitative animals. From the cradle to the grave, we learn to do what we see others doing. In fact, our most profound and lasting lessons are not formally taught but are absorbed simply by observing those around us. This process is called *cultural conditioning,* and it is so subtle, yet so all-encompassing, that unless we are incredibly self-aware, we never even know it is occurring.

What is Culture?

Culture in the sociological sense is not associated with refinements in society, such as the arts, music, literature, or appealing architecture. Nor is it about being well-educated, or having knowledge of the best books to read or the right plays to see. Culture in the sense presented here refers to the beliefs, customs, aspirations, and myths of a specific society.

To a very large extent, our culture defines us. Who we are as individuals — outside of the innate behavioral patterns we were born with — is a creation of culture. How people express their personality is an unconscious manifestation of the conditioning instilled by culture. Much of what human beings do and know, aspire to be, or perceive as right or wrong, is a result of the culture in which we were raised. Culture quite literally determines the parameters of how we think, how we act, what our goals and ambitions are, and how we perceive others.

World-renowned sociologist Edward T. Hall describes culture's impact succinctly in his landmark book, *Beyond Culture,* when he states, "There is not one aspect of human life that is not touched and altered by culture."[1] However, individuals are rarely, if ever, aware of behaving in accordance with culture's conditioning, primarily because that programming has been so ingrained in our being that we are inseparable from its influences.

Language and Culture

A powerful example of the impact of culture in our lives is how we learn the language of the nation in which we are raised. This process starts at a very early age, prior to any formal education. As children we intuitively absorb language by observing those around us and mimicking them. We are encouraged and guided along the way, certainly, but most of what we learn is through observation and then repeating what we have observed.

We absorb culture in much the same way. We intuitively learn our native culture, just like our native tongue, through the process of unconscious observation, absorption, and imitation. In fact, while learning the proper way to verbally respond to specific stimuli, we also learn how to behave in those situations. And if we happen to step outside of what is considered appropriate behavior or language, our caregivers will generally suggest a more culturally acceptable action or response. This process of enculturation molds us into expressing ourselves through specific cultural rules and regulations, and is something that continues throughout our entire life.

As Amitai Etzioni states in his treatise on culture and society, *The New Golden Rule,* "Infants are born physically human, but are psychologically, socially, and morally animal-like."[2] That is to say, human beings are animals until we learn, by absorbing the proper modes of cultural behavior, how to act appropriately. In essence, it takes other people to teach us how to be civilized human beings. Or as anthropologist Clifford Geertz states: "Without men, no culture; but equally, and more significantly, without culture, no men."[3]

A country's culture is of paramount importance to the development of each person's human potential within that society. So much so, that what we think of as "personal preferences" have actually been deeply conditioned into us by our culture, without our even realizing it. Everyone within a specific culture is a unique individual, but the choices we make, in most cases, do not extend beyond accepted cultural norms.[4] Each person is an individual, but the way we express our individuality is defined for us by our culture.

How does all of this relate to sprawl? Where we live, and the manner in which we are raised, dramatically influences how we behave, which in turn influences the development of our culture.

As suburbia is the foundation upon which our society has been built, it has had a profound impact on the socialization of most Americans. As the majority of us have been raised in the isolated surroundings of suburban sprawl, we have missed out on the shared experiences that are essential ingredients for developing into respectful citizens.

Certainly, courteous interactions do occur in America; however, in general, because our urban landscape separates us from others, many of us have not learned how to relate appropriately in public. We have forgotten how to treat one another with mutual respect and kindness. As a result, our national conduct has degenerated to the point where abrupt and impolite behavior has become the norm.

Individualism in America

Without the central cores of small towns or neighborhoods bringing people together, sprawl has splintered America into an atomized nation of individuals who feel little allegiance to the whole. Individual expression has always been part of American society, but it has rarely been undertaken at the expense of others or to the detriment of society as a whole. From its inception, America was molded by a culture that valued freedom and individuality. Historically, this country was settled by people who needed to be self-starters, who could tackle the wilderness without being told what to do. Americans learned to protect, feed, and educate themselves without an institutional entity guiding or directing them. However, as Ronald Gross and Paul Osterman point out in their book, *Individualism: Man in Modern Society,* this independent behavior always took place within the context of community.[5]

Of all the American myths, none is more powerful than that of the trail-blazing individual or family moving west on their own. However, nothing could be further from the truth! Unfortunately, the *Little House on the Prairie* books and television series have falsely bequeathed us an image of the self-reliant pioneer family. Americans have come to believe that pioneers heading to or settling in new land out west did not need help from anyone. Despite this misguided perception that the frontier was filled with rugged individuals, frontier life was actually firmly rooted in the interdependence of community.

As social historian Stephanie Coontz points out in her groundbreaking book, *The Way We Never Were,* prairie farmers owed their survival and economic success to a vast government apparatus of land grants, military protection, and investment in new lands. But more importantly, Americans relied on an extensive network of fellow settlers who supported one another by sharing resources, helping with cabin raisings, hay collecting, butchering, harvesting, threshing, and every other aspect of life on the frontier.[6]

Dependence on community support has been the rule rather than the exception in American history. From the very beginning, Americans have defined themselves within the context of a cohesive society. Despite their differences, people looked out for one another. Pioneers moving across great distances and settling in uncharted landscapes, threatened by numerous and unknown dangers, banded together because they needed one another. There was, of course, the occasional lone traveler and individual explorer. But in the vast majority of cases, to cross and settle the wild continent safely, one traveled with a group.[7] Such an adherence to community was a necessity; it was also a natural expression of the human need to belong.

Simply put, human social character is fixed in our biological nature. We have evolved to need a connection to community. Throughout the two million years of human evolution, we have lived in communities. Certainly, we have constantly strained against the compulsion imposed by our "tribe," yet at the same time we have been driven by the need for identity within that group. As a rule, these conflicting desires have been adequately mediated and accommodated, and the dominance of one to the complete exclusion of the other has usually been unthinkable — until now. Suburban sprawl is the first time human beings have lived isolated and alienated from community life at such a coordinated, societal level. The impact is dramatic.

Prior to modern times, Americans conformed to the group and actively sought out its membership, while also maintaining and expressing their individual needs and desires. Extreme individualism was usually held in check by people's connection to others in genuine communities. This in turn fostered a sense of responsibility to the whole. The independent, self-reliant nature of Americans was rarely at odds with a need for community.

Until the prevalence of sprawl, American culture did not espouse the type of individualism that exists today, where people indulge their impulses or express themselves regardless of the impact on others. Today, America's taste for self-reliance is no longer tempered by a physical landscape that connects people in communities.

Sprawl has sliced through the moorings that traditionally connected Americans to each other, and has set adrift those values that extend beyond the self. To an extreme unparalleled anywhere else on the globe, American culture has been transformed into one where people attempt to exalt themselves individually, unconnected to the rest of society. Because of sprawl, and the isolating, anti-social culture it has spawned, American society has been so radically altered that private desires have almost completely supplanted public values.

The "Me Generation"

Many sociologists and writers, as well as average citizens, have been noticing this change in American society, how it has become ruder, more demanding, less understanding, more insolent, and less accommodating. Even at the formal gathering places of work and school where strict rules of behavior exist, people's civility has declined dramatically. Americans may be polite to their friends, family, and sometimes their coworkers, but when interacting with people in public many of us have become downright rude, without even knowing that we are.

Many of those studying this breakdown have noted that our nation's discourteous cultural expression began with the "Me Generation," those people born between 1945 and 1961. These people also happen to be the first generation of Americans raised in sprawl — the first to be socialized outside the cohesion associated with genuine communities. At the risk of oversimplification, this generation has been labeled as overly selfish, constantly pursuing individual aims and immediate gratification, demanding more and more "rights" while refusing to accept responsibilities.

Certainly, we are all born self-centered, needy, and irresponsible. Babies have only one thing on their minds — themselves. Feed me, warm me, soothe me. However, children learn to expand their world view as they grow older, learn to take other people into account, learn to share. Regrettably, the development of this expanded consciousness, awareness and concern for others outside of immediate family and friendship groups, has been severely curtailed by sprawl. Without genuine communities teaching us the lessons we need to be a part of a civil society, America has been transformed into a country defined by individual pursuits, not collective concern. Many of us now act as if the world revolves around us, indifferent to the needs of others, selfishly focused only on our own personal desires.

As the pace of life quickens, and as we continue to be separated and isolated in the anonymity of suburban sprawl, many people no longer practice the politeness their parents may have instilled in them as young children: "If you can't say anything nice, don't say anything at all." "Respect your elders." "Do unto others as you would have them do unto you." Leslie Charles, author of *Why Is Everyone So Cranky?,* observes, "We have lost not only our civility, but all tolerance for inconvenience."[8]

This breakdown in society is reflected in a poll taken by *U.S. News and World Report,* which indicates that Americans think their country has become a nasty and rude place in which to live, where disrespectful behavior, uncouth drivers, foul language, and unruly kids now hold sway. Eighty-eight percent of respondents said lack of civility is a serious problem in our society, over 90 percent felt that incivility contributed to violent crime, and 80 percent said the problem has worsened in the past 10 years.[9]

Cycle of Incivility

A good example of the breakdown in civility is the way many of us tend to interact with retail employees, frequently treating them as mere functionaries of the economic cycle, not like "real" people at all. Because we don't see them laughing with their families and friends at a restaurant, working on their houses, or riding the bus to work with us, they are only workers, here to serve us. Because of their anonymity, they might as well be ATMs for all the respect many of us show them, and they us.

For their part, clerks often spend their time talking among themselves, complaining about work, gossiping about friends, or yakking on a cell phone, while at the same time attempting to process customer orders. Encounters such as these are neither respectful nor civil. And when they occur, many of us treat these uncivil retail workers rudely in return, which only increases their insensitive behavior. Thus begins a cycle of incivility that gets passed from one person to another. This spiral of misbehavior turns victims into retaliators, instigators into victims, innocent bystanders into collateral damage and once-pleasant public encounters into battlegrounds.

We all consider ourselves to be basically "good," but haven't we ever lost our patience with a clerk or waiter and then been embarrassed when we found that someone we knew was watching? Even good people tend to be less good when we're not around people we know, or are not establishing (or maintaining) a relationship with someone.

Because we are all strangers in sprawl, we are all more likely to act badly even if we are good people. In the anonymity of sprawl, we are all intuitively aware that we are unlikely to ever again see most of the people we encounter. As a result, it is easier to be rude to one another. The dislocated landscape of sprawl helps to create a self-perpetuating cycle of incivility.

Disruptive Students

Another manifestation of the American culture of disrespect is that students are arriving on college campuses unversed in the subtle art of public interaction. Students now disrupt classrooms, insult and threaten teachers, talk during class, leave noisily before lessons are over, forcefully question grades, and generally run roughshod over any semblance of academic courtesy. "The problem is much worse than it was," says Jack A. Cranford, an associate professor of zoology and ecology at Virginia Tech. "I think the incidence of this in the last ten years has doubled, if not tripled, in terms of the amount and the severity."[10] His opinion is shared by many other university officials. As a result, mandatory workshops on politeness, civility, and appropriate behavior are now being taught in schools all over the country.

However, rude behavior does not start in college. Fran Donaldson, an educator for over 20 years and now principal of Deep Run Elementary School in Howard County, Maryland, is shocked by the discipline problems she witnesses today as compared to 20 years ago. She has had children spit on her, kick her, and trip her. In one school week, a third-grader upended his desk and shouted obscenities at his teacher; a fourth-grader kicked another girl in the back; a fifth-grader told his teacher to shut up; and a first-grader exposed himself.[11] These are not isolated instances. The behavior of children all over America has deteriorated rapidly in the past few decades. Hill Walker, a University of Oregon professor and director of the Institute on Violence and Destructive Behavior, is quoted in *The Washington Post* as saying: "The things I'm hearing and seeing [in the classroom] now are so unheard of it's shocking."[12]

Emergency Vehicles Ignored

Incivility has gotten so bad that even emergency medical vehicles are being ignored. An increasing number of people are not moving out of the way of ambulances and fire trucks. District of Columbia fire chief Donald Edwards describes the situation like this: "There appears to be some sense of apathy on the part of many of the motorists, who will not stop or yield to any emergency apparatus."[13] Laura Trujillo, of the *Arizona Republic,* wrote in DrDriving.org that fewer and fewer people today are pulling over for emergency vehicles and "firefighters say it is much worse than it was just ten years ago." A special report aired July 13, 2001, on KFMB TV News out of San Diego, focused on how more local drivers were ignoring emergency vehicles.[14] Such socially abhorrent behavior is not restricted to the roads. According to the Association of Flight Attendants, rude, even criminal, behavior is sharply on the rise during flights.[15]

Rudeness Studies

Due to this rather obvious trend toward incivility, a nonpartisan, grassroots movement advocating kindness and generosity in public and private life called Americans for More Civility has emerged. This group was co-founded by former *Abilene (Texas) Reporter-News* editor and author Glenn Dromgoole and Alan Gibson, author of *Priceless Gifts: Simple Ways to Make a Difference in the Lives of Others.* The basic premise of the organization is that without civility, a healthy society does not work, no matter how splendid its constitutional guarantees or how robust the economy.

Their movement has gathered steam in the past few years, and universities such as Harvard, Johns Hopkins, and the University of California agree that the pair may be on to something. All three universities have commenced academic programs and courses of study designed to look into civility and how it affects society.

Others have noticed America's decline in civility, including Stephen L. Carter, author of *Civility: Manners, Morals, and the Etiquette of Democracy,* who writes about an "incivility crisis" that threatens to tear our society apart, and Ignacio L. Götz, professor of philosophy at Hofstra University, who puts it very clearly in his book, *Manners and Violence,* when he says, "We live in a culture of disrespect."[16]

Things have gotten so out of hand that for strangers to coexist amicably rules of behavior must now be clearly posted in public places. Health clubs display codes of conduct informing members not to monopolize workout equipment or take up too much bench space in locker rooms. Public transportation systems post signs telling people not to spit, play loud music, floss their teeth, clip their nails, or apply their make-up out of respect for others. Movie theater management and patrons have to plead with people to be quiet during shows. Restaurants and theaters are increasingly forced to implore customers to turn off their cell phones. Magazine and newspaper articles informing people how to interact as civil members of society are now commonplace.

Combating rudeness has even become a cottage industry. Companies offering consulting services to help foster civility in the workplace are in high demand, and for good reason. An article published in the *Journal of Occupational Health Psychology* reported that 71 percent of polled federal workers said that in the past five years they had been the recipients of one or more incidents of workplace incivility, defined as rude, discourteous behavior and a general lack of regard for others.[17] Offenders include the "parasite" who thoughtlessly rattles on about personal problems, the "elitist" who passes others in the halls but ignores them completely, the "time bomb" who explodes at any provocation, the "complainer" who sours the work environment with caustic views, the "slob" who has lamentable hygiene, the "egg shell" who cries at the drop of a hat, or the "slanderer" who does not hesitate to stab others in the back.

Writing in the *Academy of Management Review* in 1999, two other researchers noted: "Historians may view the dawn of the 21st century as a time of thoughtless acts and rudeness: we tailgate, even in the slow lane; we dial wrong numbers and then slam the receiver on the innocent respondent; we break appointments with nonchalance."[18]

The Media's Influence

The mass media has played a prominent role in the socialization of every American, particularly since television's commercial inception in the 1950s. In the process it has contributed greatly to creating our current culture of incivility. Whereas parents, teachers, and clergy once presided over the socialization of the young, the popular mass media culture is now the main influence. Television, film, music, cyberspace, and the celebrity culture of sports and entertainment now dominate the process of shaping attitudes and beliefs. In a very short period of time, entertainment sources have replaced the guidance once engendered by our communities and core social institutions.

Previously, our ideas about life were shaped by the members and leaders of our communities. Now commercial media enterprises establish our fundamental understanding of society, public life, obligations to each other, and even the idea of what it means to be an American. Our culture is now being force-fed to us by the media via television and other forms of electronic enter-tainment. This control over our country's culture has happened so quickly and is now so pervasive mainly because without gen-uine communities to counterbalance the media's influence, Americans have limited alternatives for socialization.

Many studies have indicated that the continuous airing of dis-courteous behavior on TV translates into the same sort of actions in real life. In both 1972 and 1982 the US Surgeon General's office conducted comprehensive reviews of existing research into the media, and in both cases found an undeniable link to antiso-cial behavior.[19] This is because human beings are hardwired to imitate what we see others doing.

One of the most fundamental aspects of this uncivil influence is the media's open display of rude behavior. The media is now so saturated with the guttural and vulgar that it has become impossible to go through life without confronting images, lan-guage, and behavior that once would have filled us with deep shame and embarrassment.[20]

Rochelle Gurstein, a professor of history at the Bard Graduate Center in Manhattan, notes that in the late 1980s, Americans expressed shock when the Clarence Thomas hearings raised con-cerns about soda cans and pubic hairs. But the Clinton-Lewinsky scandal a decade later seemed small potatoes in comparison.[21] And that involved semen-stained dresses and cigars used as dil-dos. Led by the media, our society is fast degenerating down a coarse and crass path. Many of the messages the media beams at us are a continuous indoctrination into brazenly independent, unconstrained, and radical behavior, which usually means disre-garding and disrespecting others.

We are frequently told by advertisements to "Have it your way," "Break the rules," "Have no fear," "Be yourself," and "Just do it."[22] Concern for others plays no role; only our own individ-ual gratification matters.

The "Survivor" television series and other reality shows are prime examples of this "winner take all" attitude. These shows are generally not about people working together to overcome adversity for the benefit of all; they are about raw competition between individuals. The group does not matter; the individual must win at all costs.

We are also faced with "shock jocks" on the radio, individuals who are paid to insult anything and everything. Talk shows have turned into bloodbaths, where a full complement of rude behavior is expressed. Something must be askew in society when a show such as Jerry Springer's tops the TV ratings charts. Even intellectual panel discussions, such as "The McLaughlin Group," often culminate in uncivil displays where guests end up yelling at one another. And many scenes from the popular sit-com "Seinfeld" were simply about the best way to creatively insult others.

This media-induced incivility is the most consistent and frequent message many of our children — and many of the rest of us — ever receive. While watching or listening to these shows, we are being subtly but actively programmed to believe that such behavior is acceptable. Searching for guidance, striving to fit into society, attempting to learn proper behavior, but increasingly cut off from positive human interaction, we are being socialized by the media more and more. In fact, according to Conrad Phillip Kottak, in his book *Prime-Time Society,* "by the end of high school, [each American] will have spent 22,000 hours in front of the [TV] set, versus only 11,000 in the classroom."[23]

The Three Musketeers would be laughed out of town if they were around today. The concept of "one for all, and all for one" would be considered ridiculous. As would John F. Kennedy's statement from the more recent past, "Ask not what your country can do for you. Ask what you can do for your country." Instead of being concerned about the public good, all we seem to be looking out for is number one.

Certainly, the role of entertainment has always been to challenge and stretch standards of behavior. But with no genuine communities to counterbalance the modern entertainment industry's effect on society, the Hollywood version of reality becomes the accepted one. Without communities to temper the media's influence and socialize people in the subtleties associated with positive interpersonal interaction, rudeness has become rampant in modern American society.

The very act of viewing television — just sitting there and staring while ignoring everything else around us — has also negatively modified the behavior of Americans who have grown up with TV as their main socializing agent.[24] Instead of learning how to behave through a continuous stream of healthy interactions with others out in the real world, Americans now learn inappropriate social patterns through the isolated process of viewing television.

For example, when watching TV people often get up and leave the room at will — behavior that is then re-enacted in the company of others. It is not unusual for individuals to enter and leave conversations, ignoring other people as if they were an inanimate television set.[25] And, as mentioned earlier, college students are displaying an increasing tendency to enter and leave classrooms whenever they want.

Further, since the TV is always on, Americans have learned to tune it out while doing other things. This same behavior is used around other people. Take the time to notice how many of us now ignore others, whether in conversation or walking down the street, almost as if we have pressed the mute button on a remote control.

Often we avoid even looking into other people's eyes. When passing others on the street, or even when involved in a face-to-face transaction at a store, many Americans avoid eye contact. We would rather study the counter, wall, sky, or ground than engage one another with our eyes.

At the same time, if we do happen to catch someone's eye, these people will often glance away quickly or stare blankly, with no acknowledgment that they have actually been seen. No nod, no smile, nothing. We are now so rude to one another that many of us do not feel we need to even acknowledge the presence of others.

Constant television viewing and separation from genuine community interaction has helped foster an antisocial illusion of omnipotent control. As Kottak describes it, Americans are now "imagining that they can freeze, fast-forward and reverse not just video images but also reality."[26] All of this increases rudeness and incivility and reduces everyone's quality of life.

Along with the influence of the mass media, many theories have been offered to account for Americans' increased rudeness. These include video games, latch-key kids, a consumer culture that promotes instant gratification, parents setting poor examples, schools not doing their jobs, and religious groups not being proper guides. All of these may certainly play a role in perpetuating the loss of civility in America, but the root cause of rudeness is right in front of us every day. It's in the roads we drive on, the lack of community space, the absent urban cores, the neon strips surrounded by parking lots, the lack of viable public transportation, and the overall fragmentation of our physical landscape.

As professor John F. Freie points out in his book *Counterfeit Community*, the decline of public spaces has precipitated a decline in civility and tolerance for others.[27] Continuous community interaction in public spaces would provide arenas where individuals could practice and learn sociability and respect for others. For good reason, many experts from the fields of environmental psychology and psychogeography believe that communities are the key factor in taming rude, self-centered impulses. Where we live clearly impacts how we behave.

Suburban sprawl has created an alienating urban environment, which in turn has spawned this crisis of incivility in America. Sure, we are nice to our friends, family, and in most cases even our co-workers, but generally many of us tend to treat others with disdain.

CHAPTER FOUR

A Breeding Ground for Violence

> Man is the most formidable of all the beasts of prey,
> and indeed, the only one that preys systematically
> on its own species.
>
> — William James

ISOLATION AND INCIVILITY ARE NOT THE ONLY PROBLEMS we face in America today. Frustrated by the rude behavior they encounter, people are turning violent. All over America, average citizens are losing their cool, blowing their tops, and attacking each other. Leo the dog is thrown into California traffic in an expression of road rage. One Massachusetts father beats another to death in a fit of anger at their kids' ice hockey game. Every year there are an estimated 3,000 to 5,000 "air rage" incidents where passengers become violent or belligerent while flying on an airplane.[1] There is "restaurant rage," where customers irritated with slow service lash out angrily and become violent. At the mall, "parking lot rage" contributes to fights over parking spaces, or vehicles being severely scratched in retaliation for someone pulling into what the perpetrator perceives as "their" spot.[2]

David Kupfer, a Falls Church, Virginia, clinical psychologist specializing in anger management, reports that the last decade has seen a steady increase in the number of public displays of violent anger.[3] Ignacio L. Götz, professor of philosophy at Hofstra University, points out in his book *Manners and Violence* that the country's increase in violence can be directly attributed to the breakdown in civility.[4]

Recently a study by the American Automobile Association's Foundation for Traffic Safety recorded over 10,000 injuries and 218 deaths resulting from motorists who attacked one another.[5] Examples of "road rage" are legion. All it takes is one wrong move on the road and within seconds a normally mild-mannered individual becomes a fire-breathing, red-eyed, foaming maniac bent on violence. Motorists are being shot, stabbed, beaten with baseball bats, sprayed with Mace, attacked with tire irons, and run over for totally inane reasons.

Paul Eberle, in his book *Highway Terror,* takes a revealing look at the havoc caused by frustrated individuals in their cars, including such examples as a doctor chasing and then assaulting an elderly woman after she cut in front of his BMW; a teenager shooting another driver because the driver "looked at him with disrespect"; and one man killing another because "he was driving too slow." Eberle makes it clear that all socioeconomic classes, ages, and genders are involved in this epidemic of frustration, anger, and violence on our highways.

Another manifestation of the frustration associated with life in America is how frequently people have snapped, killing others, and often themselves, at their place of employment. All of these acts of rage seem to be clear indications that something is inherently flawed with modern American society.

There are those who will shrug their shoulders and write these actions off as a reflection of America's historically violent nature. However, contrary to popular mythology the US has not always been a violent country. The "Wild West" was not as wild as Hollywood would have us believe. Cowboys did not go around continuously engaging in gunfights. In the ten years that Dodge City was the rowdiest cow town in the West, only 34 people were buried in the infamous Boot Hill Cemetery, and most of them died of natural causes. The shoot-out at the OK Corral became famous *because* it was so unusual.

The same dichotomy exists for the image that Hollywood has given us of the prohibition years, where the perception is that gun battles were everyday occurrences on the streets of Chicago and other cities. On the contrary, if such fire fights did happen, they were in isolated populations of gangsters, and the results were splashed all over the newspapers simply because they were so rare. Even murders in New York City up to the end of World War II, no matter how underprivileged the victim, were considered front-page fodder. Today, on the other hand, murder is so common all over the country, that it is no longer newsworthy except in the smallest municipalities.

America was not always as violent as it is today. Something happened to our society that has created what the Centers for Disease Control and Prevention (CDC) calls an "epidemic of violence."[6] Statistics make it clear that America is far more violent than it has ever been, and it is a much more violent place than other developed countries such as those in Europe.[7] What has caused this increase in violence in America?

Other developed nations have everything we do in the way of consumer toys, industrial development, and technological advancements. They have violent movies, television shows, and video games. They have pornography, drug users, prostitution, poverty, and racial disharmony. They have working parents and latch-key kids, as well as supermarkets, shopping centers, cell phones, computers, the Internet, and every other luxury we do. If you go down a checklist and compare the reasons "experts" have given for the breakdown in US society and the increase in violence, you will find that the same issues exist in Europe. However, those societies have not fallen apart as ours has.

Is there something else entirely at the root of what is happening in America? Something that exists only here and not in other developed nations?

The answer to those questions is right in front of us. The one aspect of life in America that does not exist to the same extent in Europe is suburban sprawl. Sprawl has eliminated our communities and fragmented our lives, leaving isolation, alienation, and incivility in its wake. Without genuine communities our society is disintegrating.

Other developed nations have all the negative aspects of a modern society that we have, but they have maintained the integrity of their urban landscape. As a result, their societies remain safer, more stable, and more secure. They have managed their urban growth. We have not, and we are paying the price for our negligence.

Sprawl has loosened the connection between people and untied the bonds of civility, which in turn has promoted violence in the hearts and minds of those predisposed to act upon their baser instincts. Though we may be loath to admit it, if we take the time to look at the United States in comparison to any other industrialized country, we will see that our crime rates are staggering. Even though Western Europe's population is 41 percent larger than America's, if all the rapes and homicides in Europe for the year 1990 were added together, they still do not come close to the number that occurred in America that year. Even in China, with almost 2 billion people, the number of rapes was only 50,000 — half of what it was in the United States.[8]

To better illustrate this reality, let us take one example. Our nation has almost five times more people than England, generally considered the most violent European nation. However, America had 102,560 rapes in 1990, while England's number was only 3,391. If those numbers are equaled out based on population, there would still only be 16,955 rapes per year in England. Not even close to America's 102,560! (see Figure 5.1)

The same is true for murder rates. In 1990 there were 23,440 homicides in the US, while in England there were only 669.

Figure 5.1

COMPARISON OF RAPE RATES BY COUNTRY

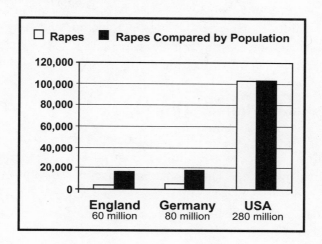

Figure 5.2

COMPARISON OF MURDER RATES BY COUNTRY

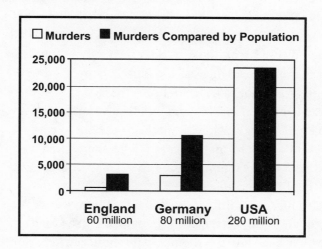

Multiply that number by 5 and there still would only be 3,345 murders in England, much less than America's total (see Figure 5.2).

These statistics make it very clear that the United States, by any calculation, and by a wide margin, is the most violent country in the developed world. We now have far more rapes, murders, assaults, and serial killings per capita than any other developed nation. Without anyone realizing it, the American dream has turned into a nightmare.

Sprawl and Violence Linked

Holding sprawl responsible for society's breakdown is as difficult as it once was to hold industrial activity responsible for global warming. The proof may never be absolutely conclusive, but there is enough strong evidence pointing the finger at both suspects that we should start taking each of them seriously.

Before sprawl emerged, America was a dramatically different country. It was safer, more livable, and more community-oriented. Certainly there was crime, but it was nowhere near as extensive or extreme as it is today. Without a doubt, other factors are involved. Nothing occurs in a vacuum. However, all things considered, the breakdown in American society and the commensurate rise in violence are too closely connected to the emergence of sprawl not to bear intense scrutiny.

Sprawl emerged in 1945 and was firmly in place by the 1960s. Not so coincidentally, side by side with the emergence of sprawl, violence in all its forms increased. The aggravated assault rate skyrocketed from 60 per 100,000 in 1957 to 200 per 100,000 in 1965, then erupted to over 440 per 100,000 by the middle of 1990s.[9] This is an increase of over 700 percent. As sprawl emerged, violence increased — dramatically (see Figure 5.3).

Another key statistic, the per capita murder rate, doubled in the US between 1957 and 1992. The murder rate doubling in 35 years may not seem so dramatic until you realize that it would be much higher if not for advances in medical technology. The actual murder rate has been held down by the development of

Figure 5.3

ASSAULT RATE PER 100,000 PEOPLE

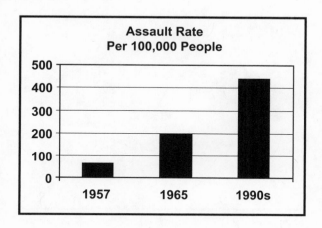

sophisticated lifesaving skills and techniques. Helicopter med-evacs, 911 operators, paramedics, CPR, trauma centers, and effective medicines all save lives that would once have been lost. According to the US Army Medical Service Corps, a wound that would have killed nine out of ten soldiers in World War II would not have been fatal to nine out of ten soldiers in Vietnam.[10] Thus, if nine out of ten gun shot victims are currently saved by modern medicine, if we had 1940-level medical technology today, the murder rate would be nine times higher than it is.

Serial Offenders

Along with having the most murders, assaults, and rapes per capita of any developed nation, the US also has the disreputable "honor" of being the serial killer capital of the entire world. Serial killings do occur elsewhere on the globe, but with nowhere near the same frequency. It may be shocking to realize that the US has 76 percent of the world's serial killers. Europe's most violent nation, England, by way of comparison, is home to only 4.76

Figure 5.4

PERCENT OF SERIAL KILLERS BY COUNTRY

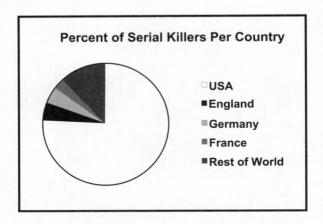

percent of the total[11] (see Figure 5.4). What is it about America that makes it a breeding ground for such violent sociopaths?

Just as with rapes, murders, and assaults, serial violence in America has not always been at such epidemic proportions. Something about America changed to lay the foundation for a dramatic breakdown in society. One factor that deserves closer scrutiny as the root cause of this change is suburban sprawl. Serial killers are an ideal test case for this hypothesis as the statistics associated with them can be tracked side-by-side with the rise of sprawl.

Between 1906 and 1959, there was a steady rate of only 1.7 new cases of serial killers every year in America. When there was no sprawl, there was no breakdown in society, and no increase in serial killers. Then, by the 1960s, with sprawl firmly established as America's main form of habitat, new serial killers emerged at a rate of five per year. By 1980, the number of new serial killers per year had risen to 15 and by the 1990s there were 36 new serial killers identified per year, an average of three a month (see Figure 5.5). Because of this increase in serial predation, the FBI has estimated that serial murders could claim an average of 11 lives a *day* in the United States in the twenty-first century.[12] The concur-

Figure 5.5

SERIAL KILLERS PER YEAR IN AMERICA

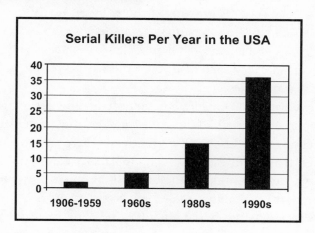

rence of the dramatic increase in serial killers and the establishment of sprawl is so striking that it is difficult to imagine why it
has not been considered before.

Serial killers are only part of the problem. The rate of sexual
assault in the US is the highest of any developed nation. "There
are a lot more serial rapists out there than serial killers," says Tom
Knowles, unit chief for the FBI's Violent Criminal Apprehension
Program (VICAP). According to the Centers for Disease Control
and Prevention, one in six women in the United States have
experienced an attempted or completed rape at some time in
their lives. The US Department of Justice reports that a woman
is raped every two minutes in the United States. Each year, about
1.9 million women in America are physically assaulted, according to the National Institute of Justice.[13]

How Serial Offenders are Created

A growing body of evidence associated with serial offenders
strongly suggests that a central aspect of their personalities is a
callous and unemotional disregard for the feelings of others. This

is something researchers believe is innate, not learned — nature, not nurture. As advances in genetics occur, evidence for the concept of a "bad seed" is growing stronger every year.[14] What this means is that a person must first be predisposed to such behavior if they are to become a violent killer or sexual offender; and every year, in every society all over the world, people are born with such tendencies.

If the only reason for serial offenders emerging is their genetic make-up, there should be the same number of such predators as a percentage of the population everywhere in the world. However, that is not the case. Only in America are serial killing and serial rape so prevalent. Hence, there must be something about America that allows these "bad seeds" to grow.

Experts who study serial offenders indicate that along with a genetic predisposition, suitable family, social, and environmental situations are also required for "bad seeds" to act on their violent tendencies. So if a person who is predisposed towards violence and/or serial predation requires the right environment to set them on their brutal path, what is that environment?

The FBI's John Douglas, an expert on serial offenders and a best-selling author of a number of books on the subject, as well as Rolf Loeber, professor of psychiatry at the University of Pittsburgh, and Felton Earls, professor of child psychiatry at Harvard Medical School, all agree that the number one factor that turns individuals into violent offenders is spending a limited amount of time with responsible, caring adults as children.[15] These experts agree that if children who are born with a genetic predisposition to violent behavior had healthy interactions with older members of society, this would help to dissuade them from acting on their predatory impulses as they grow older. Such adult interaction could be with a grandparent, older sibling, neighbor, teacher, minister, police officer, storekeeper, or youth worker. What matters is that the adult and child are able to develop a caring, nurturing, and supportive relationship that helps the child cultivate a sense of empathy for other human beings.

Such community involvement is of paramount importance, as it is now accepted by experts in criminal behavior that the desire to sexually assault — just like serial killing — has no cure once the offenders get started down their predatory path. As the FBI's Tom Knowles describes it, "Once they develop the taste for it, they want more." The only way to prevent serial predation is to stop these people from acting on their impulses in the first place.[16]

How Communities Would Help

If spending time with significant adult role models is what is needed to curtail the development of violent serial offenders, how is that going to happen in sprawl? With small town communities extremely rare because of sprawl, where are troubled children going to find the role models they need to become healthy adults?

Regrettably, suburban sprawl has eliminated the places where children can spend time with responsible, caring adults. Without the adult supervision that was so common when the majority of Americans lived in genuine communities, those who are predisposed toward violent behavior can fall through the cracks in society, descend into the darkness of their genetic makeup, and start to hunt other human beings.

Before sprawl existed, in the absence of a healthy parental figure children could depend on the whole community to be there for support, guidance, and direction. According to Richard Curwin and Allen Mendler, authors of As Tough As Necessary, "In past years, a child from a dysfunctional family had a good chance of being mentored by a nurturing adult from his or her community."[17] If a family fell apart, there would usually be another adult to fill the void — a next-door neighbor, a local store owner, or a neighborhood policeman. In sprawl, such support is virtually non-existent.

"It takes a tremendous amount of work to socialize a small human being," says Shawn Johnston, a forensic psychologist in Sacramento who has conducted over 6,000 evaluations of adult and juvenile criminals. "To cultivate a sense of empathy for other human beings, to cultivate a sense of personal responsibility, is terribly hard."[18] That work is made even more difficult in the middle of the isolation of sprawl.

Communities create healthy connections between members, demonstrating that every person has value and that other people are not objects upon which to enact distorted fantasies. Where communities exist in the rest of the world, they act as the deterrent needed to temper the onset of sexual predators, serial killers, as well as all other forms of violent behavior. However, in America today, communities are no longer the norm. We are no longer a nation of small towns and safe city neighborhoods. Instead we live in the isolation of sprawl, in places where Americans express their individuality unrestrained by the calming embrace of community life. As a result, we now suffer an unrelenting epidemic of violence. There is little doubt that the connection between sprawl and violence deserves much closer scrutiny and more serious study.

Television's Role in Violence

As was discussed in an earlier chapter, since its inception television has played a large role in socializing the American people. While it has been a major factor in shaping Americans' tastes, habits, and opinions, as well as our culture of incivility, TV has also promoted the violence that oppresses our society. Over the past thirty years, hundreds of studies have all found a clear link between violence on TV and aggressive behavior. In fact, the evidence is so strong that few researchers now doubt the connection.[19]

The most telling condemnation to date was an article by Dr. Brandon S. Centerwall in the June 10, 1992 issue of *The Journal of the American Medical Association.* The article concluded that the introduction of television in the 1950s contributed significantly to doubling the homicide rate since that time. The article emphatically stated that long-term childhood exposure to television is a major factor "behind approximately one half of the homicides committed in the United States, or approximately 10,000 homicides annually." It went on to say that "if, hypothetically, television technology had never been developed, there would today be 10,000 fewer homicides each year in the United States, 70,000 fewer rapes, and 700,000 fewer injurious assaults."[20]

That assessment is not isolated. Between 1990 and 1996 a number of prestigious medical and psychiatric groups, including the American Psychological Association, the National Institutes of Mental Health, the American Academy of Pediatrics, and the American Academy of Child and Adolescent Psychiatry unanimously concluded that TV violence contributed to violence in the real world.[21]

Yet parents continue to plunk their children down in front of the TV. Why? Because they have few alternatives. Parents cannot let their children out unsupervised. Someone might snatch them. Besides in sprawl there is no place for children to go. There are no small town squares or village greens where kids could entertain themselves under the watchful eyes of concerned shopkeepers and other community members. Without genuine communities in place to offer an alternative to the media as a source of entertainment, Americans continue to be negatively affected by TV violence.

Sprawl or TV or Both?

Television and sprawl are intertwined in modern American life. Both have a profoundly negative impact on our society. Studies clearly indicate that television is a direct causal agent of America's increase in violence; however, when sprawl was emerging in the late 1940s and early 1950s, but before television was deeply ingrained into American life, violence in all its forms had already begun to increase. Television certainly plays a role in what ails our society, but it is merely one actor on the stage that sprawl has set.

Certainly, the alienation of sprawl has created a void in our lives, which in turn has allowed us to be more deeply influenced by the images and ideas beamed at us from our television sets. However, if we had an alternative, TV would not be so influential. As noted earlier, every other developed nation can choose from a similar number of television channels as we can in America. Their citizens also have access to the same violent movies, pornography, video games, and everything else that many experts claim are causing the increase in violence in American society. However, the epidemic of violence that America is experiencing is not happening in other developed nations. Those societies continue to be stable for one simple reason: their communities remain intact.

Small town and neighborhood communities in other developed countries offer their citizens an alternative to the contrived reality of TV. Life lessons continue to be learned from other human beings, rather than from characters on television. Most importantly, bad habits imparted from television viewing are counterbalanced in the real world of genuine communities. In sprawl we do not have the option of being a part of extended communities, making us overly susceptible to the ideas and images beamed at us from television.

Both television and sprawl are connected to what ails our country, but Americans do not live in their TVs. They do, however, reside in sprawl. Sprawl is the foundation of our society. Television is not. The wasteland of sprawl is what has created the anonymity of modern American life. Television keeps us entertained in our suburban isolation, but sprawl is the reason we live in such a secluded manner in the first place. Sprawl is the reason we float anonymously through life, forced to endure the culture of incivility and breeding ground for violence that America has become.

Sprawl's connection to violence and serial predators may seem tenuous to some, but statistics and common sense clearly show a link. Cause and effect may be difficult to prove in a court of law or to replicate in a double-blind scientific study. However, as the foundation upon which our society has been built, sprawl is clearly involved in what ails our nation. The field of environmental psychology states in no uncertain terms that the physical landscape plays a powerful role in the formulation of society and its people. Assuredly, sprawl and its lack of communities may not be the *direct* cause of violence, but it is the *root* from which modern American society has grown, and that includes the epidemic of violence our nation endures. We can continue to deal with the symptoms of our societal breakdown or we can begin to acknowledge that the foundation upon which we have built our nation since World War II — sprawl — is unstable and needs to be rebuilt.

If a building's foundation were structurally flawed, it would be unthinkable just to keep adding to it — at some point, the building would collapse. The same is happening to American society. It is crumbling because sprawl has been the unhealthy foundation of our nation since 1945. For America to be a safe and civil society again, we need to recreate suburbia into genuine communities of small towns.

The statistics presented here make it evident that America's epidemic of violence emerged in lock step with the development of suburban sprawl. Before sprawl our society was as safe as those in other developed countries. After sprawl our levels of violence skyrocketed and every American's personal safety was seriously compromised.

It took over 30 years for social scientists to undertake the comprehensive studies that now clearly show a link between sprawl and America's epidemic of obesity. Even though common sense made it obvious years ago that Americans were turning into whales because they lived in a landscape that discouraged walking.[22] However, this link still took over three decades to be formally established. It would be tragic if we had to wait 30 more years for studies to show that sprawl is the root cause of the breakdown in American society.

If we continue to bury our collective head in the sand and ignore the problems that sprawl imposes on society, we are dooming our children and ourselves to a lifetime of fear and potential victimization. As long as sprawl separates us from one another, as long as we are relegated to living without genuine communities, America will remain a dangerously violent, disturbingly uncivil, and painfully alienating place to live. We ignore sprawl's impact at our peril.

PART TWO

Solutions

"Sprawl is not propelled simply by market forces. The land development and home building business sectors would have us believe that they are simply responding to the public demand for housing in general and suburban homes in particular. They lie. The housing market is remarkable because supply influences demand much more than demand affects supply. What this means is that although there is a huge fraction of Americans who do not want to live in suburban sprawl un-places, they have little choice in the market. These people want to live in true communities that are walkable, loaded with parks and other greenspaces near their homes, and where they can greatly reduce their car use."
— Joel Hirschhorn, *Sprawl Kills*

"Any massive shift in urban design will, by definition, involve millions of people making different kinds of choices about how and where they live. As a nation, we have shown time and again that we are capable of doing just that. In the last half-century alone, vast numbers of Americans have grasped the health risks of smoking and stopped doing so, creating a non-smoking culture in the process. We have learned to use seat belts almost reflexively. We have dramatically reduced incidents of drinking and driving. In what may be the most apt analogy, we have learned to recycle and agreed that the time it takes to sort our trash is a worthwhile investment in our planet."

— Kathryn Schulz, "Homeland Security Revisited," *Alternet,* January 9, 2002

CHAPTER FIVE

Creating a More Fulfilling Life

> Be the change you want to see in the world.
> — Mohandas Ghandi

THE PREVIOUS CHAPTERS HAVE SHOWN that life in America is filled with loneliness, depression, incivility, and violence. Though this is the way life is today, we don't have to continue the unhealthy pattern of seclusion, disrespect, and fear that our physical landscape engenders. Even before our government accepts its responsibility and fulfills its promise to manage our urban landscape so that genuine communities can return, each of us can take it upon ourselves to develop a more community-oriented way of life.

We have the power to choose how we want to lead our lives. We don't have to follow the herd and live anonymously in sprawl. We can get to know our neighbors and create a supportive network of caring individuals who will look out for one another. The communities we create will help to make our lives safer, less fearful, and more fulfilled. Detailed here are some suggestions that have assisted others to begin this process.

Volunteer

> Our ideals, laws, and customs should be based on
> the proposition that each generation in turn becomes
> the custodian rather than the absolute owner of our
> resources — and each generation has the obligation
> to pass this inheritance on to the future.
> — Walt Whitman

For America once more to be a healthy place to live, we need to support those organizations that continue to ease the symptoms of our country's social decay. One of the best ways to do that, and to reconnect with our communities at the same time, is by volunteering. Whether it's at the local farmer's market, library, homeless shelter, or park, there are many organizations where volunteers are needed and welcome. The best place to get started is with volunteer clearinghouses that offer access to a number of different projects. Such groups allow potential volunteers to try on a few groups for size until the right fit is found.

Besides helping others by volunteering, we will also benefit personally and spiritually. Volunteering will draw us out from the isolation of our home back into the community. We will feel more connected, more involved, more active, and more aware of what is going on around us. Volunteering energizes, revitalizes, and makes us happier, stronger, and more fulfilled. Time spent volunteering will turn into something we look forward to, something we will not want to miss. And one of the best volunteer opportunities, one where the need is the greatest and the impact most significant, is with after-school programs.

After-School Programs

In America today, one in five children is regularly unsupervised after school. Gina Adams, a researcher from the Urban Institute, reports that "self-care among school-age children is clearly a fact of life for millions of working families."[1] When the school day ends in America, millions of children leave safe, structured environments and are deposited into the wasteland of sprawl or the emptiness of urban blight. Without the safety and security of genuine communities, the hours right after school — before parents come home from work — are the ones where children are most likely to get involved in drugs, alcohol, violence, or sexual activity.

Because America no longer has genuine communities of shop-keepers, neighbors, friends, and family living and working around central cores, children are most at risk once they leave school. After-school programs connect kids with supportive adult role models. If both parents are working — which is increasingly the case — a quality after-school program can offer the needed adult influence to help guide children toward a healthy and productive future. High-quality after-school programs are alternatives to children spending many hours alone or with peers in unsupervised activities. Well-planned and well-staffed programs provide safe havens where children can learn and take part in loosely supervised recreation that builds strong, positive relationships with responsible, caring adults and peers. As noted earlier, this is the key ingredient to help prevent those predisposed to violence from acting on their innate tendencies.

In localities with such programs, studies by Fight Crime: Invest in Kids, a bipartisan, non-profit anti-crime organization, irrefutably indicate that children are less likely to commit crimes or to be victimized.[2] Coordinated after-school activities have been linked to the reduction in the juvenile crime rate, and it has been shown that it is less probable that adolescents will engage in risky behaviors, such as smoking or drinking, when they have after-school programs to go to. Also, when involved in after-school programs, children watch less television. Since many studies have linked violent and aggressive behavior with TV viewing, this could also help to reduce violence.

Successful after-school programs also strengthen the cohesiveness of the entire locality by building partnerships with local businesses and the civic community. These partnerships replenish our urban environment and help to recreate communities in America. After-school programs began to help children, but they have ended up helping people from all walks of life and from all different segments of society. After-school programs perform a necessary service in a society devoid of safe, central cores around which genuine communities can exist.

The need for these programs is not going unnoticed. Congress funded the 21st Century Community Learning Centers initiative by appropriating $200 million for after-school programs in 1999, up from $40 million in 1998. In his 2000 budget, President Clinton allocated $600 million to support approximately 5,000 centers that will serve close to two million children.[3] President Bush has continued these initiatives with his support of the "No Child Left Behind" program.

By helping to weave localities together, volunteer activities such as working with after-school programs have become America's first tentative step toward recreating the sense of community that has been missing from our lives for over fifty years. Whatever we decide to do, our volunteer experience will be a step toward a more fulfilling and rewarding life, while also helping to make America a better place to live.

Seek Out Niche Communities

> What life have you if you have not life together?
> There is no life that is not in community.
>
> — T.S. Eliot

Even if we do not live in a small town or city neighborhood, there are still plenty of other ways to find a meaningful connection to others, even if it is only in niche communities. Though not nearly as satisfying as comprehensive, genuine communities; organized, formal gatherings with people who share similar interests can ease the isolation and alienation of sprawl. Whether it is bicycle enthusiasts who spend their free time churning out the miles and burning off the pounds, literary types who organize book clubs, or people who gather to play their favorite instrument, niche communities are everywhere. To be a part of one usually only takes going to their next meeting. Then before we know it, we are part of a community of people who enjoy the same things we do. Getting involved with a group is just as complex, fun, and adventurous as a new relationship. And just as significant. Which means it is important to take our time, screen a few groups, and find one that fits before we make a commitment.

Start Your Own

If there are no groups that appeal to our unique set of interests, we can start our own! If we enjoy playing Ping-Pong and can't find a club to join, but the local community center has some Ping-Pong tables that nobody seems to use, we can start a Ping-Pong club. One way to generate interest would be to organize a tournament. Those who participate form a pool of possible members for our new group.

Or say our interest is armchair travel. We simply adore reading travel guides about specific countries and comparing the merits associated with each. Obscure, yes; but who's to say that there aren't others out there who wouldn't enjoy the same thing? The best place to search for such a club is at a local bookstore, preferably one that's independent and owner-operated. First we can ask the owner or manager if she knows of anyone with the same proclivity. If so, maybe she can put us in touch with them. If not, ask if a gathering can be held at her store. The pool of people who participate in the meeting can be the beginning of a niche community.

Another excellent way to find community, this one closer to home, is the tried and true method of organizing a block party. Naturally, we will need to get to know some of our neighbors first, which may entail actually walking over to their homes, ringing their door bells, and saying hello. These social calls could also be recruiting visits. Organizing a block party is a big job. It's best to have people working together. Otherwise the organizer would end up overwhelmed. Once the organizing committee is established, we have already created a niche community. The block party itself will then extend our connection to others in the neighborhood.

Find Your Own "Cheers"

Another ideal way to instill a sense of community in our life is to find our very own "Cheers," a place where everyone knows our name. The first step involves starting to frequent a local coffee shop, restaurant, diner, or café on a regular basis. The best places are those where other locals already gather. The way to find such hangouts is to go to a number of different establishments around where we live, and see which ones are the most popular, or are frequented by the types of folk we could get along with.

After selecting our "Cheers," the next step is to start making a connection with the people who work there, most importantly the owners or managers. Do this informally, over an extended period of time. By becoming a regular customer, being friendly to the wait staff and other patrons, our face will become known, and eventually our identity will as well. Be aware that this might take some time if one is not the effervescent, outgoing type. Eventually, however, we will be recognized and welcomed as part of the community.

Community Barter

As modern life continues to get increasingly complex, accomplishing even the most fundamental tasks seems to entail paying for services. Whether it is getting our lawn mowed, the house painted, or finding a babysitter for our children, in most cases we end up hiring someone to do the job.

Instead, we could consider creative ways to share the responsibilities of life with our neighbors. There is a big difference between having a neighbor mow our lawn in exchange for watching her children one afternoon, and simply writing a check for a landscaping company. There's a personal connection in the former scenario that is lacking in the latter. Bartering interactions such as these are the essence of creating supportive, sustaining community life.

Establishing a community barter system can help create what Co-op America calls a "circle of support." They suggest helping people become connected to others by establishing "exchange networks" in our neighborhoods.[4] Anne Slepian, former editor of the *More than Money Journal,* proposes doing this by organizing a "Neighborhood Exchange" gathering. She did this by coordinating a potluck dinner where everyone wore name tags printed with the one thing they wanted to trade and the one thing they needed. As the potluck progressed neighbors agreed to swap their goods and services, such as home repairs, lawn mowing, computer help, and babysitting. The ultimate exchange was the creation of a strong sense of community.[5]

Today in Anne's Arlington, Massachusetts, neighborhood the Internet has broadened the reach of their community barter system to include the overall Arlington area, allowing for a more extensive system of exchange. Even so Anne and her neighbors still hold regular potlucks, continuing to solidify their bond of community.

Certainly each of these suggestions takes time and effort. But this is what we must do if we want to be a part of something other than our immediate families and friends. Without genuine communities offering us the ability to connect with others informally on a main street, in a piazza, or at the village green, it is up to each of us individually to create formalized situations so that we can become a part of others' lives. So let's turn off our TVs, get out of our homes, and start to make those connections that will enhance our lives.

Participate in the Farmers' Market Phenomenon

> Such prosperity as we have known ... is the consequence of rapidly spending the planet's irreplaceable capital.
>
> — Aldous Huxley

Being a part of what I call the Farmers' Market Phenomenon is a great way to connect with our local communities. The way to do it is by rejecting the anonymity of chain stores and shopping at locally owned stores or local farmer's markets. Where we spend our money has a profound influence on how our urban environment gets structured. Consciously choosing commercial transactions that help the local economy will contribute to the preservation of local communities, while also connecting us to them.

The Farmers' Market Phenomenon is sprouting all over America. Markets are popping up everywhere. According to the US Department of Agriculture (USDA), the number of farmers' markets has grown dramatically, increasing 79 percent from 1994 to 2002. There are now over 3,100 operating in the United States.[6]

Farmers' markets create a central focus point for the community. In farmer's markets we are in a convivial environment, walking among and interacting with our neighbors while shopping. As well as offering fresh produce, farmers' markets also serve up healthy doses of community. By shopping for food the old fashioned way — by going to market — people are expressing their need for social interactions.

A huge chain store supermarket may offer us a better price on a pound of peas; but in terms of community and vitality, forget about it! Farmers' markets beat huge chain stores hands down. In comparison to farmers' markets, a chain store is sterile and lifeless, the antithesis of community.

Most importantly, by frequenting farmers' markets we will be helping to maintain a way of life — that of the independent family farmer —that is swiftly disappearing under the bulldozer of sprawl and the dominance of corporate factory farms. As large corporations continue to swallow up family farms and turn farmers into contract workers, agribusiness has become a contemporary feudal system in which farmers have been relegated to the status of modern-day serfs on their own land.

Regrettably, this is not just happening to farms. The same fate is befalling independent, owner-operated businesses. When a shopping center comes to the outskirts of a small town, the main street dies, and with it all the independent businesses as well. The people who once owned those stores, who were independent businessmen, entrepreneurs living the American dream, now have to become wage earners beholden to a corporate aristocracy.

Without anyone seeming to realize it, the US has turned into the land of corporate free enterprise, rather than the land of the free. Small businesses are now more widespread in Europe than in America. Citizens in European countries are now better able to determine their own futures than we are. This is an ironic twist, as many of our ancestors fled Europe to escape oppressive aristocracies that reduced an individual's freedom. We are ignoring our ancestors' legacy by allowing large corporations such as Wal-Mart to limit our own self-determination and become our new feudal lords.[7] Yet we support such a system of covert oppression whenever we shop at chain stores; the money we spend there deprives small shops and farmers of the revenue they need to survive. We can keep the spirit of freedom alive by shopping at farmers' markets and local stores. This will help keep local small farmers and shopkeepers economically viable and help them to make a stand against the oligarchy of corporate feudalism that is dominating our country.

Similar to farmers' markets, local stores are also focal points around which communities develop. Local stores are smaller and are usually run by the owners or a few committed individuals. These proprietors are dedicated to helping us have more than a shopping experience: they want us to feel welcome and well-served. By shopping at small local stores, we will come to know not only their owners or managers, but also our fellow citizens who shop there. Shopping locally may cost a little more, but that little extra money pays to connect us to the place in which we live.

Some huge box-like chain stores attempt to mimic this feeling of being recognized that exists in smaller stores by having "greeters" at the front door. These people say hello to us as we walk in, but we all know it is forced friendliness. They are paid to say hello; they never learn our names. We may be greeted, but we are never recognized or truly appreciated, as we would be in a smaller, independently-owned store.

Efforts are underway to raise awareness about this issue. On November 20, 2004, independent businesses in two dozen cities joined forces to urge residents to "unchain" themselves by patronizing only locally owned stores and restaurants that day. The event, dubbed America Unchained, was organized by the American Independent Business Alliance (AMIBA). The goal, according to AMIBA's director, Jennifer Rockne, was to enhance awareness of the local economic benefit of choosing to shop at locally owned businesses instead of chains.[8]

There are so many ways to spend our money more wisely and help our communities in the process. We just have to start looking beyond the glitter of the neon strip. Every dollar we spend is a vote for a way of life. We can spend our money at anonymous chain stores and ensure that our neighborhood or town will be devoid of character and community. Or we can buy locally and cast our vote for a more sustainable, healthy, and community-oriented way of life. The choice is ours.

Suggestions for Community Engagement

> Our society is not a community, but merely a collection of isolated family units.
>
> — Valerie Solanas

Being a functioning member of a genuine community is not an experience many people in America have ever had. As a result, it seems appropriate to supply some simple rules for participating in one. These suggestions are very general; they do not apply to all situations, but in the majority of cases will help individuals ease themselves out of the anonymity of their individual lives and back into the warm embrace of community life. These guidelines are not written in stone. Actually, they should be broken on certain occasions. In fact, that's the first rule.

Use Your Own Judgment

Though we may be a newcomer to a niche community, that does not mean we should always defer to more experienced members' impressions of what is right and wrong. We can rely on their knowledge, certainly, but still make up our own mind. Take, for example, the situation of joining a bicycling club. We can defer to someone who knows what is needed to ride 100 miles without collapsing, but we should always do what makes us feel comfortable.

We can respect the wishes and desires of others, but decide for ourselves how far we want to go in whatever activities the community participates in. There is nothing wrong with standing up for ourselves, as long as we do not do it in a domineering, authoritarian sort of way. Learn to bend, while standing firm, like a sapling in a strong wind.

In essence, we have free will. If someone is attempting to impose their will, no matter how amicably, without our consent, we can use our best judgment, then take a stand or take a hike. There are always other niche communities to belong to.

Trust But Verify

In general, it is always better to be polite than to be a jerk. However, at the same time, it is important to be able to trust the people with whom we are interacting. Maybe these people's personalities are not compatible with ours. Maybe their morals and values do not jive with ours. Becoming a part of others' lives in a community is a heart-warming experience. But it is always best to know who we are dealing with. Which means that it is best to take our time getting to know other community members before committing ourselves too deeply.

Don't Get into Petty Altercations

Life is too short to fill it with misplaced anger. Being a part of a community means being adaptable and amenable. If someone does something we do not appreciate, getting angry only makes matters worse. Learn to take a step back before responding to a situation. Get rid of the need to be right, or assert your will on the situation. Take a deep breath, count to ten, let the moment pass. However, if the situation keeps cropping up over and over again, either confront it respectfully, or find another niche community.

Have a Sense of Humor and Perspective

The best way to avoid altercations is to have a sense of humor. If something bad happens, imagine that it is a couple of days later and you are looking back on the moment. From that vantage point, most things are not as serious as they initially appear. Laughter is the best medicine. Learning to laugh at oneself is even better.

Besides a sense of humor, having a sense of perspective is also important. If someone is acting a little persnickety, they could be having a rough day. We all go through tough moments. Try to be understanding and non-judgmental. Smile and move on. Realizing that all things pass, makes all aspects of living, whether in a community or not, much easier.

Ask Questions

There is no better way to learn about a community or its members than by asking questions. Think like a reporter. It is amazing what people will reveal if someone is willing to listen. Be aware, though, that being an active listener is a humbling experience. It helps us realize that our ideas and views are not always how others feel. Listening also helps us to understand that we don't always need to be the one talking, the center of attention, or the perceived expert. Learning to ask intelligent questions and listening instead of imposing our ideas on a gathering will go a long way to connecting us with others.

Be Generous

Most people feel obligated to repay someone who has given them something. Instead of paying back favors, why don't we agree to take a person's generosity and pass it on to someone else? Instead of paying it back, pay it forward. This creates a web of connection and assistance that extends far beyond a simple exchange between two people. It helps to develop a cycle of civility, counterbalancing the rudeness and lack of community that pervades our entire society.

Attitude Adjustment

> The community and family networks which helped sustain earlier generations have become scarcer for growing numbers of young parents.
> — Bernice Weissbourd

One of the best ways to create community in one's life, without organizing an event, joining a club, creating a niche group, or finding your own "Cheers," is to simply alter in small ways how you deal with others in public. Instead of staying in a sprawl-induced shell, avoiding contact with others, you can start to go out of your way to connect with them.

Be pleasant. Smile. Make eye contact. Greet others, even if you don't know them. Whether walking down the street and passing by a stranger, or buying something in the mall from a clerk, make eye contact, smile, and greet them verbally in a pleasant way.

Next, and this is the key to the puzzle, have absolutely no expectations about those people maintaining eye contact, smiling back, or returning the greeting. In all likelihood they won't. Generally, they'll avert their eyes. Suddenly the ground, wall, or the scenery will become mesmerizing. It is amazing the lengths Americans will go to avoid looking each other in the eye. A return greeting may only come out as a grunt. On top of that, we may get a look indicating that these folks think we just did something very distasteful. Or they may simply stare blankly, looking right through us.

That's OK too! Let it go. Remember, by being polite and friendly and making an effort to connect with others you will be acting in a way that has not been considered normal in America for a long time. So just accept others' conduct for what it is — an unconscious manifestation of their culture — and try not to get upset or stop trying.

The best rule is to be patient. No, be really patient. Be really, really patient. Imagine you are doing this for yourself. You are saying hello and smiling to make yourself happy, not to get a reply from anyone.

In doing so you will not only make your life better; you will also enhance the quality of life of others without them even knowing it. How so? Just as people's negative attitudes create a cycle of incivility, so too will positive behavior begin the process of creating a cycle spinning in the opposite direction, one of civility. Acts of friendly politeness will rub off onto some of those to whom it is directed. Think of it as a gift. Those people in turn, some of them anyway, will take our gift and pass it on.

Your actions will begin to perform an attitude adjustment on those around you. Maybe not right away, but eventually you will become a positive force in the creation of community in your own life, as well as the lives of others.

Move to a Community

> Town life nourishes and perfects all the more civilized elements in man.
>
> — Oscar Wilde

If changing your attitude isn't working, and you can't seem to find the right niche community, think about moving to one of America's few remaining small towns. Or if you are more adventurous, US cities are going through a dramatic revitalization process right now and many urban neighborhoods have become, in a very short period of time, great places to live again. You can also find, generally deep in the heart of sprawl, the growing development trend called New Urbanism that builds places that mimic the layout of small towns. Another community-oriented way to live is called cohousing — intentional communities of private residences combined with shared public space. There are a number of community-oriented options out there. It just takes some effort on our part to find them.

Small Town Life

Even though most small towns have been almost completely eradicated by sprawl, some still exist, albeit far removed from major metropolitan areas. There are places such as Corning, New York; Keene, New Hampshire; Asheville, North Carolina; Astoria, Oregon; Galveston, Texas; and many others that have all been able to maintain healthy small town cores, vibrant main streets, and a cohesive sense of community. These are ideal places to raise a family and dramatically improve your quality of life. By being more rooted in community, you will no longer feel anonymous. Doing errands, going for a walk, or heading to work, you will continuously run into people you know. This sense of recognition is powerfully therapeutic, a complete contrast to the isolation and alienation of modern American suburban life.

Some of these remaining small towns are a uniquely American phenomenon called college towns. Nowhere else in the world are there so many towns so dominated by institutions of higher learning. In most countries, universities are predominantly located in major metropolitan areas. In contrast, many US colleges and universities are situated in places with fewer than 100,000 residents.

College towns such as Ann Arbor, Michigan; Charlottesville, Virginia; Middlebury, Vermont; and Iowa City, Iowa, are still great places to live, mainly because the schools have kept the towns focused. As an institution, it was important for the university to stay compact and centralized. This helped to maintain the integrity of the urban spaces around each school, keeping the small towns themselves vibrant and healthy.

One possible drawback to living in these towns is that fewer economic opportunities are available. Jobs are generally not as plentiful and wages are not as high, although that is not always the case. However, in these out-of-the-way locations, the cost of living will also be dramatically lower, and most importantly, the quality of life will be much higher than anywhere in sprawl. For information about college towns refer to "College Town Life" in "Appendix C: Resource List." For small towns, in the same appendix refer to The National Trust For Historic Preservation and its annual list of "Dozen Distinctive Destinations."

City Living

If we don't want to give up a full range of economic opportunities, but still want to escape the anonymity of sprawl, we can always move back into a city or an older inner suburb. Living in these places will allow us to walk to stores, school, restaurants, work, and entertainment, increasing our contact with neighbors. This will help to eliminate the paralyzing sense of loneliness that permeates living in sprawl.

Cities cater to families from all walks of life and socioeconomic backgrounds. Cities offer more options, freedom, and mobility than can ever be experienced in sprawl, and as such are vast playgrounds for both children and adults. This is especially true now, as urban revitalization is sweeping the country and many people are moving back into America's cities.

In sprawl, parents are isolated with their children in the nuclear family, completely separated from the resources that could enhance their lives. In a city there are stores, entertainment, and the company of other people right outside the door or within walking distance. The geographic proximity of amenities in a city integrates people into a collective life filled with opportunities for self-expression and personal and communal fulfillment. Instead of being surrounded by total strangers, as we are in sprawl, in urban areas we meet neighbors and make new friends on our walks to the zoo, museum, local playground, corner store, café, bus stop — wherever we go. The proximity of everything and ease of access is also powerfully liberating for parents, as it mitigates the need for them to chauffeur their children everywhere.

There is one major obstacle stopping people from moving to cities or closer-in suburbs: the perception of the quality of public education. It is true that many US cities are currently saddled with underperforming public school systems that do little to prepare children for the complexities of a modern, technological future. As a result, many parents opt to move out to the suburbs once their children reach school age.

With urban revitalization, however, more and more families with school-age children are continuing to live in urban areas. These people are the vanguard, the trendsetters in their generation, combating stereotypes and cultural programming, and they are having a dramatic impact on inner city schooling. These parents are pushing school systems to enhance the learning environment, improve safety, and increase test scores. They are demanding more educational resources, better teachers, and more challenging courses. As a result, in every American city there are now good schools that prepare students in nurturing and safe learning environments for a productive future. If more parents continue to move back into cities and take the time to improve urban schools, the tide will continue to turn, and our cities will come back to life after being left for dead in the 1950s and 60s.

New Urbanism

Another option besides relocating to either a city or small town is to move to a New Urbanism development in sprawl. Many of these places combine all the elements of traditional small towns, including a main street with stores, small offices, parks, apartments, schools, and other public buildings. From this central core, housing for many different economic levels radiates out, allowing a genuine, diverse community to evolve. New Urbanism developments in Celebration, Florida, or Kentlands in Germantown, Maryland, are popping up all over the country. They are wonderful options for people unwilling to make the leap back to the big city but who desire the connectedness and safety associated with living in a community.

Just as in small towns, in many New Urbanism developments people can walk to do their errands and go for a stroll in the evening to the local ice cream shop, coffee bar, or restaurant. For entertainment they can amble to the movie theater or see a play at the community center. Swimming pools, tennis courts, and other recreation facilities are all within walking distance. This freedom to walk, along with having informal gathering places, helps people connect with one another, laying the foundation upon which genuine, livable, and safe communities are built. For information about New Urbanism developments refer to "New Urban News" in "Appendix C: Resource List."

The success of these projects is shown by how popular they have become. One of the most famous New Urbanism small towns is Seaside in the Florida Panhandle. Born with limited fanfare in 1983, the average price for a home was only $65,000, easily within reach of lower-middle class salaries of the time. In 2002 however, the average house in Seaside sold for almost $1 million, a rise of over 1,400 percent.[9] If this increase in value, in the span of only 20 years, is not a clear indication of the demand for places that are built with community in mind, I am not sure what is.

Cohousing

Another community-oriented option is called cohousing. Cohousing projects are intentional collaborative residential developments designed and managed by the residents, where the people involved are consciously committed to living as a community.

This unique development style combines the best features of private housing with the warm embrace of community. In cohousing, private dwellings coexist with common spaces for group cooking and eating, meetings, laundry, play areas, guest facilities, and other amenities that can be shared by the whole community. Community in cohousing is there if desired, but people can also retreat to the privacy of their own space.

The typical cohousing project has 20 to 30 single-family homes along a pedestrian street or clustered around a courtyard, creating a community-oriented neighborhood. Some are in apartment buildings in inner-cities. Cohousing residents include doctors, lawyers, engineers, stay-at-home parents, urban planners, teachers, graphic designers, writers — a large cross-section of society.

Since the late 1980s, cohousing has developed successful examples of conscious communities all over America. Currently, there are more than a hundred such communities completed or in development across the country. For more information about cohousing developments refer to the Cohousing Association of the United States in "Appendix C: Resource List."

My only caveat with cohousing is that it has the potential to be exclusive, like a gated community, rather than inclusive like a genuine small town community. Despite these misgivings, until the government begins to fulfill its covenant to build safe places where communities can form, cohousing is an option to consider, as are New Urbanism developments, and relocating to cities, inner suburbs or small towns. Many Americans are consciously choosing community over the alienation of sprawl. Why not us as well?

Unplug From the Media

> I'll tell you what's wrong. We're lonesome. We're kept apart from our neighbors. They want us huddled in our houses . . . watching television

because they can manipulate us then. They can make us buy anything, they can make us vote any way they want.

— Kurt Vonnegut, Jr.

Though Kurt Vonnegut's statement may seem slightly extreme to some, he's not far from the truth. Television is one of the main catalysts for individual isolation in America. By remaining glued to the television every night, alone in our homes, we eliminate the possibility of connecting with others. Television, as well as other forms of electronic entertainment, has made it increasingly possible for people to cut themselves off from everyday life and pursue a segregated world of their own.

Ever since the fragmented physical landscape of sprawl eliminated easy ways to interact with others, television began to take over the social life of America. Without genuine communities, the fictional world of television quickly became America's surrogate community. The fantasy world of TV has become such an all-pervasive aspect of American life that television characters have increasingly taken the place of real human companionship. Television programming plays a more powerful role in our lives than many of us realize.

TV Addiction

Television is an almost omnipresent companion to most Americans. Many people I know schedule their lives around their favorite TV programs. They rush home to view them, curtailing whatever real experiences they are having for the fantasy world of TV.

"Not unlike drugs or alcohol, the television allows the participant to blot out the real world and enter into a pleasurable and passive mental state. The worries and anxieties of reality are as effectively deferred by becoming absorbed in a television program as by going on a 'trip' induced by drugs or alcohol," asserts Marie Winn, author of *The Plug-in Drug*.[10]

The essence of any serious addiction is the pursuit of pleasure, a search for a "high" that normal life does not supply. That is exactly the allure offered by television. Says Winn, "The television habit ... renders other experiences vague and curiously unreal while taking on a greater reality for itself."[11]

Classic addiction is also characterized by the inability to function without the addictive substance, a dependence on the addictive experience. Television viewing fits that classic indicator of addiction, as most people cannot imagine living without their daily fix.

At the same time, just as heroin addicts neglect other aspects of their lives when they stick needles in their arms, TV users also avoid real life when they plug into their fictional realities. TV viewing is extremely isolating socially. The process of watching television weakens relationships by reducing and sometimes eliminating normal opportunities for communicating.[12] Television effectively reduces interpersonal connection simply by the amount of time people spend sitting in front of it.

"Just as alcoholics are only vaguely aware of their addiction, feeling that they control their drinking more than they really do, people similarly overestimate their control over television watching," continues Winn. "Even as they put off other activities to spend hour after hour watching television, they feel they could easily resume living in a different, less passive style."[13] But most never do. They say they will. But instead, they remain plopped on their sofa, glued to the TV, and life goes by without them.

No one wants to admit that they may be addicted to the distraction of television. We just want it, that's all. More of it. All the time. We can't imagine living without it. But that doesn't mean we're addicted. Does it?

Whether we are addicted or not, Americans seem unable or unwilling to live without their televisions, and for good reason. There is little of interest directly outside people's homes in suburbia. TV has filled the void left by the absence of genuine communities.

The fragmentation of our physical landscape and the resulting lack of genuine communities has kept people isolated from one another, which in turn has made us overly susceptible to television's lure.

Life After TV

We are currently living in an age of technological advancement that distracts us from what really matters in life — community, family, and friends. Television as a public medium has only been available for about 60 years. In contrast, humans have inhabited the planet in one form or another for over two million years — all without television. That life was not a bland existence. Before the advent of TV, at the end of day's work, people did not simply sit in front of a fire and stare at it. Life was more active and revolved around other people. Whether eating, drinking, talking, singing, dancing, making love, or storytelling, people found plenty of activities for entertainment.

Today the same could be true. We could read a book, go for a bike ride, learn an instrument, play with our kids, make new friends, go for a walk, volunteer, coach a sports team, write letters, give a back rub, take a luxurious bubble bath, paint, draw, take a class, plan a holiday, and so much more. Unplugged from the TV we could resume the life we've been neglecting since television became the focus of our free time.

When we finally do unplug and start connecting with others again, uninterrupted by the random voices and images beamed at us from the box, we will start to feel an expanded inner self, a clearer understanding of issues, and a broader vision of life. Since our attention will not be spread so thin as a result of constantly distracting media intrusion, our immediate world will suddenly become that much more compelling. By spending less time in front of a television, the characters on a sitcom or the action in a sporting event will be of less importance than the people in our immediate life. Real life will start to hold more value than the fantasy world of TV. By opting out of a steady diet of media distractions, we will finally be able to see the possibilities that life has to offer.

Once free from television's clutches, we will slowly start to see what we have been missing. Just as when one is freed from the control of a chemical drug, circumstance will look more refreshing, more welcoming. There will be so many more opportunities available. We'll have more time on Saturdays and Sundays, because we won't be glued to some televised sporting event. Our evenings will be free again, because we won't be planted on the sofa in front of a sitcom. Freeing ourselves from television will allow us to get involved with our community and family, and become more active physically and spiritually. A life without television is the first step toward actually having a life.

Just Say No

Television is a powerfully addictive drug with a profound influence on people's lives. Whether that influence promotes violence, isolation, or incivility, the only way to fully understand how television and the mass media guide our lives is to free ourselves from their coercion. Not only from the TV, but from radio, movies, magazines, and the Internet as well. Only by spending more time away from them can we see how they have narrowed the focus of our lives away from issues that are important to our health and well-being.

By eliminating, reducing, or monitoring television's influence in our lives, we will have a much richer, more fulfilling existence. So turn it off, or better yet unplug it. Keeping the TV unplugged reduces the temptation to turn it on. Another effective way to reduce television viewing is by placing a decorative cloth over the set. Keeping it out of sight helps to put it out of mind, reducing the desire to turn it on.

Whatever method we use to begin the process of weaning ourselves off television, we should start as soon as possible. Life is waiting. (To find out how to wean ourselves off of TV, refer to the listing for The Center for a New American Dream in "Appendix C: Resource List.")

Get Out of Your Car

> Restore human legs as a means of travel.
> Pedestrians ... need no special parking facilities.
> — Lewis Mumford

Automobiles are extremely effective barriers to community engagement. By confining ourselves in rolling steel and glass boxes we cut ourselves off from potential human interaction. Not only is it an economic imperative that we reduce our dependency on automobiles — remember the $500,000 we could save over a lifetime mentioned in Chapter 2 — but it is also a social and communal necessity. How can we interact with others if we are speeding by them in our cars? How can we get to know our neighbors if the only way we encounter them is bumper-to-bumper rather than face-to-face? Automobiles may have increased our mobility, but they have also increased our isolation. If we want to change the course of our lives and enhance our sense of fulfillment, maybe it's time to start getting out of our automobiles. Listed below are five suggestions on how we can get out of our cars and back into our communities:

1. As pointed out in more detail in a previous section, if we really want to break free of our car, it may be necessary to move to a place where a car is not as much of a necessity. Urban areas fit that bill.

2. Where public transportation is available, start taking it to work. If local public transport is adequate, using it is by far the easiest way to reduce the car's impact on our lives. On the subway or bus going to and from work we can relax, read, think, meditate, plan the day and meet people — everything we can't do in a car.

3. Give up the automobile addiction completely and go car-free. Living without a car is not only liberating, it is easy, as long as we live in an urban area with extensive public transport. And

if we need a car, for whatever reason, we can always rent one. Going carless is not for everyone, but if the circumstances are right, and the desire is there, giving up our car is possible.

4. Begin biking or walking to do errands. Once we remove ourselves from our automobiles, it is amazing how easy it is to connect with others. Cars tend to isolate people, but walking, biking, or rollerblading can free us to meet other people.

5. We can use a car less often and in more creative ways. Car sharing is one such example of creative automobile usage. Car sharing is freeing thousands of urban dwellers from the burden of car ownership, giving them the convenience of being able to drive when they need to at a fraction of the price. More than 70,000 people now belong to car-sharing groups in at least 300 towns and cities in Europe and North America. Such programs are most successful in areas that are overwhelmed by sprawl and have an established group of urban residents, such as Boston, Seattle, and Washington, DC, where programs already exist. In such locations car-sharing can be a part of the multifaceted transportation system that America will need in the near future.

Once we get out from behind the wheels of our cars, we will start to realize that there is more to life than getting frustrated in a traffic jam. Not stagnating in gridlock will free our souls, reduce our stress level, and make us happier, healthier, and more fulfilled.

Civility Needs To be Taught

> Every man is a creature of the age in which he lives; very few are able to raise themselves above the ideas of the time.
>
> — Voltaire

In America, without communities in place to informally educate us, we are all being subtly indoctrinated into the culture of incivility that permeates our society. The only way to combat the tyranny of our uncivil cultural programming is to formally teach people a different way to behave. Whether that is in school or at home, proper rules of social interaction need to be demonstrated and reinforced for healthy interactions to occur in public. By teaching the young to be respectful, we will be able to sever the continuity of the culture of incivility that, since sprawl emerged, has flowed through the generations.

In Schools

To achieve this re-education of society through our children, our schools will need to lead the way. This means that almost everything about the way we educate our young will need to be changed. By recreating the overall environment of our schools to include lessons on respect, and offering living examples of how to show respect to others, we can begin the process of derailing the new American culture of incivility. By educating our young in the proper rules associated with behavior in society, we will start to steer America back to becoming a civil society once again.

Our schools will continue teaching our children to read, write and do their 'rithmetic. However, one more "R" will be added to that list: Respect for others and oneself.

At Home

No matter how significant a student's school life, much of what they learn still comes from the home. To return our country to being a civil society again, we need to reinforce a school's lessons in respect by instituting similar teaching at home. Unfortunately, today many parents do not even realize that their kids are being disrespectful. And even if they do, many do not do anything about it. For any number of reasons, parents today impose few rules on their children; as a result children are not learning to control their impulses, which eventually leads to rude behavior. Being a parent means being a benevolent disciplinarian. Avoiding doing so will relegate our children to a lifetime of anti-social behavior. A few suggestions that parents can use to help children learn the proper way to behave include:

- Emphasize the need to say "please" and "thank you" without being prompted.
- Discourage children from interrupting conversations; let them know they are not the center of the universe.
- Teach children how to introduce themselves to adults: how to stand up, look an adult in the eyes, extend their hand, and come out with a polite greeting.
- Develop verbal and non-verbal cues to let children know they're acting rudely.
- Don't try to reason with children who have yet to develop their full reasoning capability; stick with your initial admonition, repeating it as often as necessary.
- Impose swift, logical, and understandable consequences to uncivil behavior.
- Watch your own speech and actions; make sure you model politeness at home and in public.

Politeness and manners also can be taught to our children through hospitality, showing gratitude, learning to respond to invitations, and good sportsmanship. Polite behavior has to be taught, over and over again, until it sinks in. Attempting to change a rude culture one person at a time will be a daunting task. However, we need to start somewhere. And, if not now, when? And if we're not going to do it, who will?

CHAPTER SIX

Creating a Healthier Society

> We must have towns that accommodate different
> educational groups, different economic groups, dif-
> ferent ethnic groups, towns where all can live in
> one place.
>
> — Margaret Mead

A FTER TAKING THE INITIATIVES OFFERED in the previous chapter to recreate community and civility in our lives, the
next step is to convince our local and national representatives to reverse many of the urban and transportation policies
that have been implemented over the past 60 years (see
"Appendix A: How Sprawl Came to Be") and which have done so
much to diminish the livability of our nation and the safety and
well-being of its citizens. When these radical alterations of the
landscape were being made, few individuals could envision the
impact that highways and urban "renewal" would have on inner
cities, or the effect that unplanned suburban sprawl would have
on small towns. However, it has become increasingly obvious
that where we live and work, instead of representing the American
dream, has instead been twisted into a nightmare.

Ever since sprawl emerged, violence has increased, depression and suicides have reached epidemic proportions, and incivility has become rampant. Suburbia, while initially seeming to enhance quality of life, has really only helped to erode it.

We need to bear in mind that things do not have to be this way. The existence of sprawl is not pre-ordained. It can be changed. We have it in our power to alter the forces that are creating sprawl. However, we must first become aware that there is a need for change. Next, we must work to enact some fundamental changes in how we manage our society. What follows are six activities that can help make our society healthy and livable again:

1. Professionally manage our urban spaces
2. Diversify our transportation system
3. Increase the gasoline tax
4. Change zoning laws to allow small towns to be built
5. Change tax laws to stop promoting sprawled development
6. Vote in local and national elections to ensure that all of this can happen.

To be brutally honest, despite the need for Congress to act on all of these suggestions, it is unlikely that anything will happen anytime soon unless we, the citizens of America, do something about it. The political influence of the highway lobby makes any discussion of what Congress should do largely academic. For the most part, those who hold political and economic power will initially have little interest in creating genuine communities, as such places would reduce their power and influence.[1] By keeping us isolated from one another, those in power are able to maintain the status quo, a situation that has been economically lucrative for them, but socially demeaning for us. Despite this predicament, if we make our voices heard in the electoral process, I remain confident that America will emerge from the quagmire of sprawl and become a healthy, safe, and community-oriented place to live again.

Manage Growth

> Growth for the sake of growth is the ideology of the
> cancer cell.
>
> — Edward Abbey

The government created the current land use rules that reduce the incentive for real estate companies and commercial lenders to build anything other than sprawl. Well-managed, cohesive, multi-use developments that would help communities grow are not part of our current zoning regulations. Sprawl is now, and has been for quite some time, the only legally accepted form of development in America.

To say it another way, our current zoning laws actually make it illegal to build small towns (see the "Change Zoning Laws" section in this chapter). If a developer wants to build a multi-function suburban development complete with shops, restaurants, cafés, homes, and apartments, the regulatory process for getting local government approval for such a place is often too long and arduous for builders to even bother. Banks that finance urban development projects, whether residential or commercial, are very leery of even considering mixed-use development for the same reasons. Time is money. The more time wasted on trying to get laws changed to build a quality place to live, the less money a developer will make. As a result, American developers focus their energy on building sprawl, and small towns are no longer created.

The majority of suburban developments prior to 1945 were self-contained small towns with all the functions of life specifically built within walking distance. Prior to sprawl, the federal government played a role in ensuring that livable places were built. Suburbs were constructed based on well-established protocols, including mixed-use development patterns and a variety of housing types.

However, after World War II, federal, state, and local governments abandoned flexible and sensible urban planning and replaced it with restrictive, isolating, community-destructive zoning. This lack of vision needs to end. We need to start managing our growth through coherent and comprehensive urban planning. By doing so, we can once again create small towns complete with central cores and main streets, from which genuine communities can develop and grow.

Managing growth will not only give us the impetus to change the degrading development patterns of sprawl, but it will bring us back together as a society. People will be able to walk, bike, or take safe and efficient mass transit to places within their own towns or to other urban cores. By managing growth we will be creating places where people feel safe and have a sense of belonging, rather than empty wastelands that evoke the current atmosphere of emptiness, anonymity, and fear.

Because of our rapid population growth, we should have been managing our urban expansion more than other countries; instead we did less. According to the US Bureau of Census, between 1950 and 1997 America's population increased by 116 million. It is anticipated that our population will grow by 60 million more by 2020, and reach 571 million by 2100.[2] If we keep sprawling without coordinating this growing population, our society will become even less livable and more dangerous. In the long run, our economy will stall because of the drain that sprawl imposes on our resources and our lives. It's time to start managing our physical landscape to accommodate the people we already have and the millions more that are flocking here every year to share in our economic success.

Urban Planning

Whether we call it New Urbanism, Managed Growth, Neo-Traditional Development, Transit-Oriented Development, Historic Preservation, Traditional Neighborhood Development, Smart Growth, Garden City Development, or just common sense, we need to better manage our urban landscape. "Plan well and you have a community that nurtures commerce and private life," Al Gore said during his presidential bid in 2000. "Plan badly and you have what so many of us suffer from first-hand — gridlock and sprawl."[3] It is time that we returned to traditional neighborhood patterns of livability — compact grids of streets and blocks with a mix of housing types and commercial and civic buildings, all developed on a human scale and well-suited for pedestrians and social interaction.

However, urban planning is more than just creating places to live, work, shop, and entertain. True urban planning, as it is done in Europe, entails the integration of transportation, environmental concerns, and farmland protection on local, regional, and national levels. Each of these areas impacts the other, and none should be approached without considering the rest. According to historian Mary Hommann, "Urban planning has been capable, in control, and ongoing in European democracies for almost half a century, demonstrating the kind of difference planning could make in America if similar legal policies were adopted."[4] In the United Kingdom, for example, there are fewer than ten regional shopping centers. This is in a country of 60 million people. Once it was clear that such places destroy town centers and suck the life out of cities, the British government simply put a stop to these projects.[5]

This is but one example of how other countries' governments support the needs of their people instead of allowing business interests to run rampant over the populace. Here in America, on the other hand, shopping centers continue to be built, and our government, on all levels, ignores the negative social impact of such developments.

If we just took the time to notice, we could learn a lot from England and the rest of Europe. It appears we almost did. In 1969 we started down the path to rational urban planning when the National Committee on Urban Growth Policy urged the construction of new towns as the way to better coordinate future suburban expansion. This committee cited efforts by England and Scandinavian nations since World War II that successfully combined transportation and urban development to create bucolic small town settings.[6]

As a result of this committee's effort, in 1970 Congress passed Title VII of the Housing and Urban Development Act, which authorized a program of mortgage insurance to aid and encourage the development of new towns.[7] Unfortunately, this initiative was doomed to fail because it envisioned that a private developer, all by himself, would be responsible for all aspects of planning and developing a small town. Congress failed to realize that government is the only entity that has the resources to marshal all the forces needed to change the zoning laws required to build a small town, connect it with public transit to other locations, organize the police force and fire protection, and build the sewer systems, schools, hospitals, and libraries that create a fully functioning small town. To imagine that one lone individual could successfully create a viable small town in the 1970s was ludicrous. America was no longer a frontier nation where towns emerged almost overnight without government involvement. Nor were the 1970s the Gilded Age of the late 19th and early 20th century, when obscenely wealthy individuals such as Henry Morgan Flagler, co-founder of the Standard Oil Company with John D. Rockefeller, actually did have the power and money to create towns from scratch. Flagler did this throughout Florida so that the railroad he was building had destinations at which to stop.

It's true that in the late 1960s two visionaries, Robert E. Simon, Jr. and James W. Rouse, were able to start the process of constructing Reston in Virginia and Columbia in Maryland respectively. However, both of these individuals ran out of money well before their plans even came close to completion, turning their hoped for small towns into watered down versions of sprawl. Regrettably, the nation's lawmakers had used these two projects and individuals as inspiration to pass the 1970 bill, not realizing that they were doomed to fail.

Title VII of the Housing and Urban Development Act did not face the reality that it requires a huge investment and a long time to build a small town. Individuals, even comparatively wealthy individuals, no longer have the means for the task.[8] In established nations such as the United States, only the government with its extensive resources and power of eminent domain can acquire the land for a town, including surrounding acreage for recreation and public transportation. Only government can initiate zoning changes, and build roads, trails, sidewalks, sewers, schools, and hospitals. Only government can offer police and fire protection, inducements for businesses to relocate, housing subsidies, and a host of other services.[9] Only government can raise the money needed and take the time necessary to create livable small towns, which can take billions of dollars and decades to be fully completed. Governments at all levels — federal, state and local — need to be involved in American urban planning, or else it is destined to fail. To imagine otherwise is to live in a fantasy world.

Department of Comprehensive Urban Planning

Just as when the nation committed itself to the path of automobile dependence by enacting the National Defense Highway System in 1956, we now need to pass a bill that dedicates the nation to building small towns and city neighborhoods, promoting alternate transportation options, and recreating American communities. Just as the federal government did in 2003 when the Homeland Security Department was created absorbing 170,000 civil servants that worked at 22 agencies, so too should the government combine the efforts of agencies that currently compete for resources in the urban planning arena. Organizations such as Housing and Urban Development (HUD), Department of Transportation (DOT), Environmental Protection Agency (EPA), United States Department of Agriculture (USDA), and the Department of the Interior all work towards their own separate goals, usually without considering how their actions impact other agencies. These efforts need to be coordinated if we are going to get our country back on track. A bill needs to be passed to create a separate and distinct government agency, a Department of Comprehensive Urban Planning (DCUP), that will act as the guiding force for American community rebirth.

This new agency would be an objective, non-partisan national organization beyond corporate manipulation that would empower localities to plan for themselves. DCUP would serve as a technical and information resource for elected neighborhood, metropolitan, regional, and state planning boards, helping them to see past their differences to coordinate quality state-wide and regional plans. Information would be shared, success stories would be disseminated, and failures exposed. A process of cooperation would be created instead of the current climate of competition. Along with the advice given would come the financial resources to transform the plans into reality.

Pat McCrory, the mayor of Charlotte, North Carolina, while receiving an award from Partners for Livable Communities at a recent ceremony at the Kennedy Center, expressed the need for this sharing of ideas. "My city is as good as it is, and is getting better every day," he said, "because I borrow successful ideas from other places." The Department of Comprehensive Urban Planning would formalize this sharing of successful urban planning ideas.

An organization similar to the proposed DCUP, the Smart Growth Leadership Institute, was created to help do just that. This proactive advocacy group has brought in former Maryland governor Parris N. Glendening to help provide training and consulting services to state and local officials who want to limit suburban sprawl, preserve open space, and promote mass transit.[10] Though not initiated by the federal government, this organization has a profound potential to implement change, especially since it is headed by such a forward thinking, dedicated individual with a proven record in combating sprawl.

Another non-governmental organization (NGO) that is taking on the urban planning role that the federal government should be playing is the National Trust for Historic Preservation, headed by its president, Richard Moe. Fully funded by private donations, this organization is seeding the re-emergence of America's small towns and city neighborhoods by providing the resources necessary to create economically viable places for communities to emerge.

New Leaders

The Department of Comprehensive Urban Planning needs a new kind of urban planner such as Parris Glendening and Richard Moe to make it work. It needs people who are well-trained and intimately versed in a variety of disciplines, including architecture, environmental science, highway development, construction, sociology, psychology, and more. These new leaders must be able to think in terms of the complete, long-term puzzle, while at the same time be able to offer short-term solutions for any small problems that arise. They must be strategists as well as tacticians. They must be generalist planners as well as detail-oriented implementers. These people need to be able to envision all aspects of sustainable national urban planning, as well as to get down in the trenches and work toward achieving coherent and comprehensive solutions on a regional, local, and neighborhood level.

We need people who can envision communities not just from the narrow confines of their own limited societal upbringing but from a variety of cultural perspectives. To achieve this, new urban planners should be encouraged to travel extensively and learn first-hand from examples of successful urban environments. Most importantly, proper urban planning can only be undertaken by people who are objective, who cannot be bought, and whose principal interest is the public good.[11] We need leaders who are beyond corruption, and who are not susceptible to the influence of corporate or political interests.

America's new urban planners need to be intelligent, dedicated, determined, committed, and willing to work for the greater good. These new urban leaders must be aware of what happened to America as a result of past government policies and corporate manipulation, so that those mistakes do not happen again. They also need to be fully aware of the deficiencies of current zoning, and the importance of mixed-use developments.

The new vision of America promoted by these forward-thinking, unbiased planners would be proactive in its land use and transportation planning, and would adopt programs and policies that lead to more livable and sustainable communities. The new urban ideal would promote the expansion of transportation alternatives (high-speed rail, trolleys, commuter rail, bus rapid transit, and more), reduction of infrastructure costs, improvement in air quality, preservation of natural resources, conservation of agricultural land and open space, and restoration of local and regional economic vitality.

Without a coherent vision supported by a coordinated urban and transportation plan, the strength, vitality, and safety of America's communities, and with them our entire society, will continue to deteriorate. For America to once again be a safe society filled with pleasant towns and neighborhoods, we need to begin to manage our growth. We have spent over fifty years pursuing a vision of America that has not lived up to its billing. It is time to reorient our focus and commit ourselves to genuine communities again.

Similar to the need for clean air and clean water, having healthy places to live crosses all political boundaries. Such places would be an economic windfall for governments because small towns and livable cities would have a higher concentration of people, thus increasing the tax revenue while reducing the costs of providing services. Real estate companies, the construction industry, and a variety of other companies would also benefit, since they would be the ones creating new towns and rebuilding cities, and connecting them with mass transit. But most of all, every American would benefit, because small towns and livable cities would give us all the opportunity to live in vibrant and safe communities once again.

Blueprint for Cities

Since the infrastructure is already in place in cities, making them safe and livable again will simply be a process of restoring the landscape to what it was before highways and urban renewal destroyed it. But instead of stopping there, let's go a step further and make our cities even better than before. We have the chance to combine dynamic commercial success with vibrant urban livability. We have the space, we have the resources, and we have the technological know-how to make our cities the most livable and community-oriented places in the world. Listed below are some steps that can help to re-create safe cities and genuine communities:

1. **Eliminate or drastically reduce office ghettoes.** The core of every American city is a wasteland of office buildings. No one lives in these places. They are completely devoid of any real life. The 1949 Housing Act created these dead zones by replacing multi-faceted mixed-use communities with single function commercial zones. Let's reverse that trend by returning to an intelligent mix of office, residential, and retail space to ensure the continuous safety, livability, and economic vitality of our cities.

2. **Remove highways from cities.** Monolithic roadways slicing through our cities destroy any possible community life. Once they are removed, the neighborhoods these highways are suppressing can then be recreated. Boston, Milwaukee, and Portland have all successfully removed highways, allowing surrounding neighborhoods to re-emerge.

3. **Re-introduce mass transit.** Before highways are removed from cities, we need to implement trolley, commuter rail, or bus services such as "bus rapid transit," on a regional scale. There are plenty of successful models to follow. Boston, Chicago, and New York City have the best US transit systems, and European cities have even more successful examples, as do most cities in Canada.

4. **Eliminate empty lots and abandoned buildings.** We should require development of these blights on urban livability, or penalize the owners for their neglect. Yes, personal property is sacred in America, but we need to rethink the consequences of that cultural attitude. To create livable communities in the US, we need to reevaluate the idea that the rights of the individual should take precedence over the rights of the community. Landowners need to be made to understand their responsibility to the greater good. Lawmakers will need to use their creative genius to enact laws enabling this to occur. Such a situation already exists in Washington, DC, where the Home Again Initiative was started by Mayor Anthony Williams to take advantage of new laws giving the city more power to foreclose on abandoned properties or seize them through eminent domain.

5. **Modify large parking structures.** If large multi-story parking garages are allowed at all, have them fit into the urban landscape. Instead of letting such huge buildings dominate a streetscape without offering any benefit to pedestrians, lower floors could offer commercial and/or residential space. The way they are today, these barren monoliths create dead zones, decreasing safety and reducing community life.

6. **Create walkable cities.** Follow the model that exists in Vancouver, Canada (considered by many to be North America's most livable city), some parts of a few American cities, and all of the cities of Europe, and create city designs where urban amenities can be easily accessible on foot. If urban residents are within walking distance of vibrant central cores filled with other people, shops, offices, and public areas, this will greatly enhance safety and community life.

7. **Allow mixed-use buildings.** Multi-use structures should be created along these shopping/commercial streets, with stores and businesses on the ground floor and residential and commercial space above. This brings all the functions of life together, enlivening community interaction.

8. **Offer a variety of housing types.** In between these shopping/commercial streets there needs to be a proliferation of different types of housing so that individuals from different income levels can live near where they work and shop.

9. **Bring public services back to the public.** Public buildings — such as local police stations, schools, firehouses, post offices, and courthouses — should be established along the shopping/commercial streets. The consolidation of resources and the gigantism that has epitomized government since 1945 has separated public resources from the communities they serve. Centralized public services have economic benefits, but they bleed the life from communities by taking jobs away from neighborhoods and removing workers from where they live, all of which decreases community interaction.

10. **Tame automobile traffic.** Community interaction is impossible when streams of cars are speeding dangerously through streets. Lower-density traffic will encourage pedestrian flow, the foundation for genuine community formation. Some traffic-control methods include:
    a. Create pedestrian-only zones.
    b. Add stop signs or lights.
    c. Narrow streets so they are either one-way or one lane each way.

11. **Create public spaces.** These places could be piazza-style squares surrounded by housing, shops, and offices. Every successful city in the world has these types of places, where children play, adults stroll, and community is formed.

12. **Establish aesthetic codes.** These codes would require all developments to comply with standards of beauty and harmony; naturally, these standards would be decided on the local level by the community itself, not imposed by outside forces. For too long in America we have lived surrounded by ugly, degrading, dehumanizing, commercial architecture. As a result, we have lost touch with how important beauty is, and how

necessary aesthetically appealing surroundings are to the development of communities and healthy individuals.

13. **Conform to a specific architectural style.** Instead of letting buildings compete to be recognized as the latest architectural wonder, have streetscapes conform to a style that reflects the history and culture of the region, such as adobe architecture in the southwest or colonial buildings in New England.

14. **Rescue waterfronts.** Access to the serene beauty of shimmering bodies of water within our urban spaces needs to be available for every citizen, not relegated to industrial, commercial, or transportation use. It is time we removed highways from the riverbanks and built parks with biking and hiking paths. We need to convert waterfront warehouses into residences, stores, and restaurants. We need to consolidate shipping piers so they are shared by different companies and convert the leftover space for use by the people.

Blueprint for Suburbs

Suburbia is so spread out that re-creating communities in this environment is where America will have to be at its ingenious best. Reformulating the wasteland of sprawl will be a formidable undertaking in our pursuit of community livability and societal safety. Since we will basically have to start from scratch, recreating our suburbs will be an immense challenge.

One major stumbling block to livability in the suburbs is the existence of separate and distinct municipal governments, each lording over its own little fiefdom. The structure of American local government is such that almost every metropolitan area is divided into dozens, sometimes hundreds, of local administrative units, each mutually exclusive and often in competition with one another for economic resources. For example, there are 265 governing bodies in Chicago and 780 in New York City alone. Each of these local governments decides whether to permit new office parks or shopping malls, regardless of any burden that decision imposes on neighboring jurisdictions.

Sprawl impacts all of us, and as such it is a battle we all must fight together. We need to put aside our regional differences and partisan politics to help create livable communities all over America. Working separately we may be able to create some pockets of community livability, such as the town of Celebration in Florida, but working together we will finally be able to build livable places for every American.

We may never be able to completely erase the scar that suburban sprawl has carved across our landscape, but to make our country safe and livable again, the attempt should be made. Listed below are some steps that can be taken to erase sprawl and establish real communities in suburbia:

1. **Prune back retail-zoned land.** The current zoning technique employed by municipal governments is to designate everything along certain strips as commercial, then wait for retailers and developers to fill in the spaces. Paring back the commercial spaces zoned for retail, and allocating some of it for housing, offices, civic uses, and recreational facilities will encourage the development of small towns.[12]

2. **Transform retail strips into small towns.** There are many ways to accomplish this goal, but at the heart of each plan should be the understanding that the suburban landscape needs to be redesigned to make people feel they are part of it, not insignificant specks on its large canvas. Parking lots should be placed behind buildings, not in front of them. Structures should abut the streets, and be transformed to create an attractive and accommodating townscape. Residences need to be built nearby, and apartments placed above new commercial buildings. This will give people the opportunity to walk instead of drive to work, shop, or to entertain themselves, which will stimulate serendipitous interactions, helping to build genuine local communities.

3. **Create public areas.** Places such as parks, piazzas, and village greens should be incorporated into these new suburban towns,

creating convenient meeting spots. The public buildings of the town should be established around these public areas, including a courthouse, post office, local government agencies, and schools.

4. **Build sidewalks.** People need to be able to walk if community life is going to emerge. In current retail strips, walking is generally not an option for getting from one site to another. By encouraging serendipitous interactions on sidewalks, we can begin the process of creating community livability.

5. **Re-establish schools as community focal points.** Schools should not be isolated or fenced off from the rest of society the way they are in sprawl. Instead we need to make them part of the community again. In front of the schools would be a good spot for parks and other public areas so children can use these spaces during recess, and other citizens can use them during other times of day. This change would entail the elimination of factory-sized schools and a return to smaller neighborhood school houses. Each of these smaller schools would help create a sense of place, and an identity for residents rooted in that place.

6. **Tame traffic.** On both commercial and residential streets, walk signals need to be lengthened and roads narrowed so pedestrians can easily and safely cross streets. At the same time, routes can be built for through-traffic outside of new townscapes. By making our new suburban small towns pedestrian-friendly, communities will have a chance to form again.

7. **Rebuild the suburban landscape with aesthetics in mind.** Today, suburbia is an unappealing eyesore of cookie-cutter homes and garish neon commercial strips. New buildings should be attractive and complement each other, with a consistency of style to help create a sense of place.

8. **Establish extensive public transportation.** Systems such as bus rapid transit and/or trolleys, need to be developed linking these

new towns together. Just as importantly, bus, trolley, and/or train stops need to be incorporated into the fabric of these new towns, further helping to make them the focus of community life.

All of these suggestions to modify the urban and suburban landscapes are easily within the realm of possibility. The federal government committed the country to automobile usage and suburban living in 1945, which resulted in our country being radically changed 15 years later; a similarly dramatic change could happen with these initiatives. All we have to do is commit ourselves to this new vision for America and offer people another option besides suburban sprawl and urban blight.

Sprawl may never be fully eradicated, so it will likely always be available for those who want to live in its alienating expanses. However, for the hundreds of millions of Americans who long for the safety and sense of belonging associated with community life, comprehensive urban planning would help create such healthy places again.

Diversify Transportation

> For most Americans, progress means accepting
> what is new because it is new, and discarding what
> is old simply because it is old.
>
> — Lewis Mumford

As discussed briefly in the previous section on urban planning, transportation should not be an end in itself, pursued in isolation from other considerations. Transportation systems should be developed to help achieve larger societal goals and support the health and stability of the whole nation. Unfortunately, since the end of World War II our government has viewed transportation as an entity separate from other societal concerns such as urban planning, farmland protection, or environmental stewardship. Our government compounded this problem by supporting automobiles and airlines while allowing mass transit trolley and passenger rail systems to be illegally dismantled. Instead of making our society and economy stronger, these myopic decisions have resulted in a transportation infrastructure that is now at its breaking point.[13]

This reality was made abundantly clear when the terrorist attacks of September 11, 2001 virtually crippled the US air transportation system. After that fateful Tuesday morning Americans stopped trusting in the safety of the airlines, but when we went in search of an alternative to air travel, it did not exist. If we wanted to travel long distances in comfort, airlines were the only viable option available. In supposedly the most advanced modern society, passenger rail is nonexistent for the majority of Americans.

I am not suggesting that railroads alone could succeed in satisfying all our transportation needs. Neither can trolley lines, steamships, canals, roads, airlines, or any other single mode of transportation. No one or two transportation options alone can meet all the needs of a varied and diverse society and economy. However, that is exactly what our government has been trying to do for the past 60 years by making our nation overly dependent on automobiles and airlines. It's time to bring America into the twenty-first century by diversifying our transportation systems and including rail in the mix.

Discrimination Against Rail

Allegedly, we are the most technologically advanced nation in the world, but our passenger rail system is certainly not representative of that. The current number of passenger train routes and customers is a shadow of what it was before 1945, or even 1900. Massive government subsidies for gasoline and the operation and maintenance of highways, air traffic control, and airports — without commensurate support for rail — has relegated passenger rail transportation to third-world status in the world's wealthiest nation.

The federal government spends billions of dollars to pave roads, build airports, and deepen harbors and waterways, but railroad companies have to build, maintain, and manage their own transportation system with little assistance from the government. In 1978, an incredible $216 billion of taxpayers' money was spent on highways, $15.8 billion on air traffic control systems and airports, and only $1.3 billion for Amtrak and $2.5 billion for other public transportation.[14] Twenty years later the allocations were just as lopsided. In 1998 Congress approved a bill for over $150 billion dollars for highways, and in 1999 authorized a $57 billion spending package for airports and air traffic control. In the same bill, support for Amtrak was scheduled to be completely eliminated in 2002. Amtrak still survives, though it continues to be treated as the ugly stepchild of America's transportation system. This pattern of legislation clearly indicates how unbalanced our transportation infrastructure remains. We have been putting all our eggs in one basket without properly monitoring it; and now that basket is breaking.

Along with massive road subsidies, the government provides the majority of funding for the construction of airports by issuing tax-free government bonds. Also, most airports are government owned, operated, and free from property taxation. The government also funds support services such as the national air traffic control system and the national weather service. With the failure of private airport security, the federal government has taken over this aspect of the air transportation system as well.

The government also maintains the infrastructure of the waterways throughout the nation for the transportation of goods, and it has made them available virtually free of charge to shipping companies. Currently, up and down the Atlantic and Pacific coasts and along the Gulf of Mexico, the federal government is spending billions of dollars to deepen and widen waterways for both commercial vessels and pleasure craft users. In conjunction the government funds the Coast Guard, Customs Department and every other ancillary service needed to ensure the integrity of our borders.

These transportation systems — highways, airways, and waterways — have been deemed important enough to receive massive government support, but rail gets a pittance in comparison. For every mode of transport in America (other than trains), the government has built and maintains the infrastructure, while private companies operate the carriers on that infrastructure. For example, the government builds the roads while Greyhound operates the buses and GM manufactures the cars to drive on them. In contrast, the rail infrastructure — the tracks — are built and maintained by private freight rail companies, while the government owns and operates Amtrak. This situation forces Amtrak to lease track usage from the rail companies. If a similar situation were to exist for other forms of transport, automobile companies would maintain the road system and the government would build the cars. Airlines would run the air traffic control system while the government would operate the actual flying of the planes.

The way that passenger rail is run in this country is patently ludicrous when compared with other modes of transport. What the US government needs to do is start treating rail as it does other transportation options by building and maintaining the rail infrastructure, then allowing private companies to compete for passenger rail business using that infrastructure.

Establish Rail Infrastructure

The American people deserve to be able to experience the freedom of inter-urban passenger rail travel, one of the most liberating, peaceful, ecologically friendly, and economical ways to travel. Anyone who has traveled by train in Europe knows how relaxing and convenient rail travel is. The people who use the commuter rail lines outside Boston, New York, or Chicago also know the effectiveness of rail travel.

Studies have shown that rail is more efficient at moving large numbers of people in luxury and comfort than any other transportation option. Polls also indicate that Americans would use passenger trains if only they were more extensive and convenient.[15]

California is listening to its citizens by initiating a 20-year, $10 billion program to blanket the state with faster, more frequent train service.[16] The same is happening in the heartland. According to *The Washington Post,* the "Midwest High Speed Rail Coalition is in the advanced stages of planning high-speed rail lines through the upper Midwest," including St. Louis, Detroit, Milwaukee, and other cities.[17] Similar projects are underway or under study in Washington, Ohio, Florida, and North Carolina.

How our current rail transportation system is structured makes absolutely no sense, except in the context of the squabbles between the US government and the robber barons of the late nineteenth and early twentieth centuries (see "Appendix A: How Sprawl Came to Be"). As we enter the twenty-first century, it's time to put aside these old grievances, bring America out of the dark ages, and support rail just as much as we support other transportation systems.

European Diversification

Even after the oil crisis in 1973, America continued blithely down the path of subservience to oil. The US maintained its dependency on the automobile, while other industrialized nations diversified their transportation systems even further through rail extensions, subway additions, and increased bus service. As a result of the oil crisis, countries around the world experienced an unparalleled revival of mass transit. In comparison, the US did virtually nothing. "Since 1973, German, Swedish, French, and Canadian cities have inaugurated new suburban and regional rail systems as a response to the energy crisis, integrating them with expanded bus service along appropriate routes," writes Glenn Yago in his book *The Decline of Transit.* "Although these systems require massive infrastructure investment, they have increased the productivity of the transportation system as a whole and have reduced oil-generated balance-of-payments deficits. Other benefits included increased ridership, substantial reduction in city travel times, traffic safety increases, rising land valuations and ... environmental improvement."[18]

Europe, after three decades of seeking alternatives to oil — smaller cars, better public transit, and hi-tech wind farms that dot the landscape from Denmark to Spain — continues to wean itself off fossil fuels. We, by contrast, remain mired in the oil age. As a result, the US is strategically vulnerable to the slightest disruption of the oil supply or increase in its price. The best way to erase this vulnerability is to reduce our need for oil by diversifying our transportation system — the source of most of our oil consumption.

Oil Crisis Ahead

To fully come to grips with how important it is for the US to diversify its transportation situation, we need only recognize that all of our main forms of transportation — planes, cars, boats, and trucks — are fueled by one nonrenewable energy source: oil. This commodity is in limited supply on the planet; no major oil fields have been found since 1976 and experts suspect that there are no more to be found. Oil production is likely to peak in our lifetime.

When petroleum geologists talk about "peak production," they mean that point where half of all known oil reserves, including those projected but yet to be discovered, will be used up. After that point, the price of oil on world markets will steadily rise as oil output decreases. Estimates for when we will hit peak production vary from 2005 to 2035; but whether it is five, ten, fifteen, or forty years from now, the time is fast approaching after which using gasoline will be prohibitively expensive. This will have a dramatic impact on the world economy, but it will hit the United States the hardest, mainly because we are so overly dependent on oil.

The baby steps American companies and the federal government are looking into — ethanol and other renewable fuels, gas-electric hybrid vehicles, super-efficient diesel engines, and funding for a public-private research partnership on hydrogen power — are simply not going far enough. We not only need to find alternative fuels to run our private automobiles, we also need to focus on creating an extensive passenger rail and public transit system moved by electricity. If we do not have a diversi-fied transportation system in place, and are not transitioning into alternative energy sources when oil reaches peak production, our government's myopic commitment to oil will be catastrophic to the American way of life. Before oil runs out, it is imperative that we diversify our transportation options while we still have the economic resources to do so.[19]

Raise The Gasoline Tax

> The perpetual obstacle to human advancement is custom.
>
> — John Stuart Mill

Step number three in the plan to revitalize American communi-ties, raising the tax we levy on gasoline, will be the most difficult to enact. Only three times in the past 35 years has the US Congress increased the gasoline tax. However, despite its contro-versial nature, a gas tax is desperately needed — and makes total sense as well. Just as the federal government, through taxes, has forced up the price of cigarettes to reflect the health costs that smoking imposes on society, so too should they make the price of gasoline reflect the costs of automobile usage. (For a break-down of how expensive our automobile overdependence really is, refer to the "National Overhead Costs" section in Chapter 2.)

The artificially low gas tax in the US, besides laying a founda-tion for future economic catastrophe, is the main contributor to suburban sprawl, highway congestion, air pollution, and contin-uing our toxic dependence on the automobile. An artificially low gas tax doesn't deter people from driving, doesn't encourage the use of alternate transportation sources, and doesn't offer an incentive for people to demand more fuel-efficient vehicles. As a result of a low gasoline tax, Americans continue to use more gasoline per person than any other three developed nations com-bined. Per capita consumption of petroleum products is 459 gallons per year in the United States. The closest European nation is Germany with only 140 gallons used per person each year.[20]

Gas Tax Comparison

The graph below shows the disparity in gasoline tax and the resulting price per gallon in the United States compared to other developed nations. These figures represent prices and taxes in 2000. Every country in Europe has a gas tax rate much higher than ours, taxes which have been used to diversify their transportation systems and reduce their dependence on imported oil.

As a result of our paltry gas tax rate, at the pump we pay only between 8 and 19 percent (it depends on who is doing the study) of the overall costs associated with automobile usage. The tax money that is collected from the sale of gasoline is generally used for one purpose: to build more roads (refer to the "Highway 'Trust' Fund" section in Appendix A for more details). The

Figure7.1
GAS TAX COMPARISON

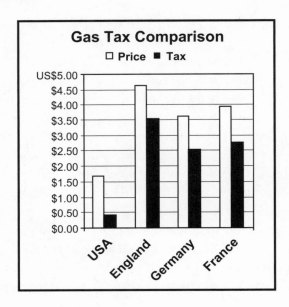

remaining costs associated with driving — maintaining roads and highways and all their relevant support systems — are covered by general, overall taxation.

Societal Benefits

Because of the way transport costs are invisibly allocated, when people are fueling up they do not realize how expensive driving really is — a situation that just encourages them to drive more. If we were confronted at the pump with the true costs of driving through higher gas taxes and thus higher prices, we would immediately be able to understand the impact driving has on our pocketbooks. In conjunction with this awareness of how expensive driving really is, over time a higher gas tax would have the following benefits:

1. **People would be encouraged to live in existing urban areas.** As the cost of living farther out and driving everywhere would be prohibitive, Americans would move back to places that are closer to jobs or public transit, promoting the redevelopment of these areas into safe, community-oriented neighborhoods and towns.

2. **New small towns would be built.** As gas prices would no longer encourage sprawled development, new suburban villages would be constructed instead, most likely around public transit rail stations. Within these suburban small towns retail, residences, and entertainment all would be in walking distance to people's homes, reducing the need to drive everywhere.

3. **Public transportation would become a realistic option.** With higher population densities in these urban cores, more people would see the benefit of using mass transit. They would begin to use what is currently available, which would in turn encourage the construction of more extensive systems.

4. **Passenger rail between cities would become viable again.** The same population densities that encouraged mass transit

would also help to promote passenger rail, as destinations would now be situated conveniently in cities, or in nearby locations accessible by public transit.

Economic Benefits

A higher gas tax would also have a positive impact on the overall economy. The construction of small towns, the rebuilding of our cities, and the development of public transit and passenger rail infrastructure would create jobs and economic growth at all levels of society, including the banking, manufacturing, and construction industries. A higher gas tax would have a positive ripple effect throughout the entire economy in a number of ways:

1. **The trade deficit would be reduced.** By increasing the price of gasoline, a higher gas tax would decrease the demand for imported oil. As oil is the biggest contributor to the trade deficit, reducing the importation of oil would dramatically reduce the trade deficit. More of our money would stay in the country instead of flooding out to oil-producing nations. In such a situation more capital would be available for business investment, helping to stimulate economic expansion and the creation of new jobs in America.

2. **The budget deficit would decrease.** The increased government revenue generated from a higher gas tax could help balance the budget. This would in turn make the economy more stable, stimulating real Gross National Product (GNP). In such an economic environment, more money would be invested and more businesses would be started, which would contribute to economic expansion.

3. Finally, **new jobs would be created** from the construction of new small towns, as well as in the emerging industries of passenger rail, public transportation, and all the ancillary manufacturing industries that supply rail cars and their supplies. More importantly, these would be good paying, long lasting, highly skilled jobs that Americans can build a life on.

Current Gas Prices Favor the Wealthy

Research by the Congressional Budget Office has concluded that the richest 20 percent of Americans use twice as much gasoline as the poorest. As the true price for each gallon of gasoline is not paid at the pump, but levied in general taxation, people who drive more have their automobile usage subsidized by those who do not. And as it is the wealthiest who drive the most, this means that the people with the most money have their transportation subsidized by those with the least. The way we tax gasoline is akin to behaving like Robin Hood in reverse: we are taking from the poor and giving to the rich.

If we raised the gas tax, those who use their cars the most would pay for that privilege. At the same time, the increased revenue could fund alternate transportation modes for those people who actually need them. A higher gas tax would take money from those who have it, to create transportation services for those who do not, so that all can share in the promise of the American dream.

To ensure that the less fortunate are properly taken care of, a higher gas tax would need to be instituted in conjunction with an expansion of public transportation. Otherwise it would be a regressive tax: the working poor would bear the burden, while the affluent would be able to pay the increase easily. If we increase the gas tax without initiating adequate mass transit, the poor will end up even poorer.

The Right Choice

We need to start looking at a gasoline tax as a direct toll paid up front by those who choose to drive. An increase in this toll would have a profoundly positive impact on every American's life. Not only would it stimulate the economy and create good jobs, but a gas tax would encourage people to move closer to urban centers instead of further out into sprawl, reducing the amount of time we spend shuttling around in our cars. This would give us more time with friends and family, help us to reconnect with a community, which in the end would help to make life more fulfilling.

Change Zoning Laws

> New ideas come into this world somewhat like
> falling meteors, with a flash and an explosion, and
> perhaps somebody's castle-roof perforated.
> — Henry David Thoreau

For over 50 years it has been illegal to build small towns in America. As incredible as that sounds, if we want to construct a place where community life exists, with a common area surrounded by public buildings, and different housing types within walking distance of a main street with shops and restaurants, we cannot. Zoning laws have segregated homes, stores, and offices far from one another. As a result, sprawl is now the only development pattern that can be legally constructed in America.

Initially promoted in 1916 by lawyer Edward M. Bassett as a way to protect the community-oriented amenities of city neighborhoods from being overrun by the onslaught of automobiles, garages, and filling stations, zoning's purpose soon became to exclude instead of include.[21] After World War II, zoning became a tool wielded by newly created suburbs to legally sanction the creation of segregated residential areas, filled only with those people who could afford to pay for that privilege. Instead of helping maintain small towns' amenities and livable neighborhoods, as was first intended, zoning quickly began to be used to stratify Americans into economic enclaves. In this process zoning was also used to eliminate businesses that would have created small towns — bakeries, delis, bookstores, movie theaters, corner stores, local pubs, and any number of other enterprises — from where people lived.

The way zoning laws are used dictates that every aspect of human activity be separated, forcing us to drive from one activity to another. It requires that community-oriented commercial activity be separated from residential activity. Zoning puts the needs of the car above the needs of the people. In such an environment, livability is unattainable and genuine communities cannot form.

Before the Second World War, mixed-use (residential and commercial) space was not only allowed, it was encouraged. In many buildings, when there was an office or a shop downstairs, the proprietor could rent the upstairs as an apartment, or would live there himself. The buildings that lined the sidewalks were ornate, elegant, and dignified. Rows of trees planted along the sidewalks made the area even more attractive. Buildings were erected with aesthetics in mind, and the entire landscape was constructed to accommodate people and the community. And most importantly, people's homes were within easy walking distance of these main street shopping districts.

However, for over 60 years, zoning has made it illegal to create such beautiful and convenient places to live. We have been zoning our suburban landscape for so long that most people born after 1930 have never lived in anything but sprawl as adults. We have always gone shopping at malls or huge supermarkets, and we have had to drive to get there. Most Americans have never lived in aesthetically appealing, community-oriented urban environments. This situation has had a profoundly negative effect on every American's quality of life as well as the health of our entire society.

Given the chance, I have little doubt that the vast majority of Americans would choose to live in small towns. However, as the construction of such places is currently illegal, we need to first change zoning laws to give this choice a chance. Only a few American metropolitan areas such as Austin, Texas, and Portland, Oregon, have adopted zoning laws that allow for what policy wonks call traditional neighborhood developments (TNDs). Not so coincidentally, both Austin and Portland are universally recognized as two of America's best cities in which to live.

For a real impact to be felt all over the country, the majority of American municipalities need to realize the importance of allowing for the creation of small towns and livable neighborhoods. We need to make mixed-use developments the rule rather than the exception. Zoning laws may be here to stay, but instead of relying on exclusionary zoning laws we could start creating inclusive ones. We could start creating zoning laws that require the creation of small towns, places that include retail and enter- tainment as well as residential in the development mix. By doing so zoning laws would begin to benefit people and communities as they were initially intended to do.

Change Tax Laws

> The difficulty lies, not in the new ideas, but in escaping from the old ones.
>
> — John Maynard Keynes

Despite all the changes that are being implemented to eradicate the impact of sprawl in our lives, one area continues to be over- looked: tax laws. Many of the misguided tax policies that created the economic impetus for the proliferation of suburbia are still in place. The two most glaring examples of this are:

1. When farmland is taxed not on its current use but according to its future real estate development potential, and

2. When the home mortgage interest deduction is used to pro- mote the construction of huge suburban McMansions.

Tax Farmland as Farmland

Because we still have tax laws that were created for the express purpose of promoting suburban real estate development, small farmers on the outskirts of American cities are still being plowed under, paved over, and pushed aside. Every single day America loses two acres of farmland to sprawl; from 1992 to 1997 we paved over more than six million acres of agricultural land — an area the size of Maryland.[22] According to *The Washington Post,* the outward growth of American metropolitan areas has eaten up 1.5 million acres of farmland each year since 1960.[23]

Since 1950, four million acres of Pennsylvania farmland alone has been turned into sprawl, an area larger than Connecticut and

Rhode Island combined. In the same time period, metropolitan Phoenix grew to encompass nearly 600 square miles, an area larger than Delaware. By most estimates, in the next half century sprawl is expected to consume more than 3.5 million acres of California's Great Central Valley, the nation's most valuable farmland, an area that supplies the majority of our produce.[24] Much of this sprawling growth can be attributed to outmoded tax laws.

When developers came calling after World War II, many landowners — usually farmers — sold their property to make large, unexpected gains on its value. Some farmers, generally the least successful, sold early in the game. These transactions, at inflated prices, raised the assessed value of adjacent property based on this new potential use, dramatically increasing property taxes on the land of other farmers.

The resultant tax burden imposed a financial crisis on the remaining farmers, whose profit margins were slim to begin with. They were raising the same crops and selling them for the same prices, but due to higher taxes the cost of owning farmland suddenly doubled or tripled. This pressure began to make it financially unviable to continue farming, forcing more farmers, often against their wishes, to sell their land to real estate developers, in a domino effect that continues to this day.

Finally, when all the adjacent land was developed, an enormous increase in the tax rate occurred, mainly because the new subdivisions needed new schools, sewers, fire protection, and other urban services. Eventually, under the increased financial pressure of higher taxes, the owners of any remaining undeveloped land had to sell or develop their property to pay the higher taxes. As a result, today we can no longer find farmers' fields, rolling hills, lush forests, or livable small towns supported by a vibrant agricultural economy anywhere near American cities. Our tax laws have made such places obsolete.

This land grab happened so fast that many people cannot even remember what life was like before sprawl. Unplanned suburban development overwhelmed the nation so quickly that the past was almost immediately erased. Today, the same pattern continues unabated.

The way to put a stop to this self-perpetuating farmland eradication scheme is to tax farmland as farmland. Quite simply, do *not* tax agricultural land as high-end commercial or residential property until and unless it has already been converted for that use. Do not base a tax assessment on the potential, future usage of the land, but on its current usage. Besides stopping the spread of sprawl, this simple measure would help to renew our agricultural security by preserving the valuable farmland we have left, while also helping to maintain the way of life of the independent American farmer. In conjunction, we would have the added benefit of preserving the natural settings that farms inhabit so that every American, now and in the future, would be able to savor the beauty of our rural heritage. Changing how farmland is taxed will do much to stop the cancerous spread of sprawl.

Modify the Mortgage Interest Deduction

Another tax law that continues to assist the spread of sprawl is the mortgage interest deduction allowable for home owners. Initially started as a way to stimulate the economy by promoting home ownership after World War II, the economic benefits of the mortgage interest deduction are now outweighed by the catastrophic social impact induced by the sprawl it has created.

How does the mortgage interest deduction promote sprawl? As every homeowner is well aware, interest charges on a mortgage loan represent the vast majority of the money paid into the mortgage. Tax laws allow borrowers to deduct those interest payments directly from their earned income. This means that the federal government is helping every American pay his or her mortgage. Which is a good thing. It promotes home construction, helps the economy, builds personal net worth, and gives people places to live. However, we all know where the largest and most expensive houses are located: out in sprawl. These giant McMansions are everywhere, all over the country, and people are being encouraged to buy these over-sized behemoths because the federal government is directly subsidizing their purchase through mortgage interest deductions.

A cousin of mine owns such a home in Grand Rapids, Michigan. He told me that one of the main reasons for buying his 6,000-foot mansion was the mortgage interest deduction. "The federal government is basically paying for half my home," he said. "I'd be stupid not to buy it." Simply put, by subsidizing mortgage interest payments, allowing them to be used as a deduction from a person's earned income, our tax laws are helping to finance the continued spread of sprawl.[25]

Tax Incentives for Community

I am not suggesting that we remedy this situation by eliminating the mortgage interest deduction. However, we should change its focus. Instead of offering a blanket mortgage deduction for any home, anywhere, we could instead offer deductions only for people who buy in existing urban areas, or in places that are being built as part of new small towns, or near public transportation stops.

All the mortgages currently in place could be grandfathered in so that borrowers continue to benefit from the interest deduction offered. However, starting on a designated date we could have new, community-focused mortgage interest deductions become law. This would encourage the creation of small towns and put the brakes on sprawl.

Another way to promote the development of small towns would be to offer a program of tax incentives to developers, encouraging them to build in existing urban areas or to construct new small towns. Such an idea is not new. Something similar was attempted in 1970 when Congress passed Title VII of the Housing and Urban Development Act. This bill authorized a program of mortgage insurance to aid and encourage the development of new towns instead of more sprawl. Unfortunately, that program never became a reality, mainly because of the flaws in the bill pointed out earlier in the "Manage Growth" section.

Even though the 1970 bill did not work, that does not mean we should not try again. However, this time let's not do it in a vacuum. Let's create a new vision of America and marshal all of our resources to promote small towns rather than sprawl. Let's create government policies that promote mixed-use development. Let's modify our zoning laws to allow small towns to be built. Let's change the mortgage interest deduction to encourage home owners to buy or build in these new small towns. Let's diversify our transportation system and connect these newly constructed small towns together, offering people the freedom to get around without a car. Let's tax farmland as farmland until it is developed, not before. Let's begin to manage our growth intelligently through the creation of a Department of Comprehensive Urban Planning. Finally, let's raise the gas tax to reflect the true cost of driving and to help pay for all of the suggestions above.

None of these ideas are unproven. They are all being implemented in other nations to successfully stop sprawl, maintain livable communities, and keep their societies safe. However, it will not be easy to implement these ideas in the United States. There are powerful forces at work here that will fight to maintain the status quo; they will do anything to ensure the continuation of laws that allow sprawl. Real estate developers, road builders, car manufacturers, oil companies, and banking institutions make hundreds of billions every year from sprawl. As a result, they have become a powerful force at all levels of our government, and they are going to continue to use all the influence their money can buy to keep change from happening.

Despite the entrenched special interests we will need to overcome, it is imperative that we alter the way we build our nation; otherwise, we will be relegating another generation of Americans to the isolation, alienation, and fear that permeates the country. It is time that we all get involved in the political process and encourage the adoption of laws to create places where communities can form. Let's vote to redesign America from the sprawled mess it has become, and return it to being a nation of small towns and livable cities.

Vote

> Government in the US today is a senior partner in
> every business in the country.
>
> — Norman Cousins

Getting our heads around tax laws, urban planning issues, and government policies can seem overwhelming. Sometimes it can feel as if the deck is stacked against us, that it is futile to try to combat the power of special interests and wealthy real estate developers. The odds may not be in our favor, but we have something at our disposal that is the great equalizer; something that others have fought and died for; something that gives the American people the power to effect change. We have the right to determine who gets elected. We have the power to VOTE.

The importance of participating in the electoral process can never be discounted. Voting is the bedrock of our democracy: a shared right and privilege that ties society together and makes our country strong. People who vote become stakeholders in their society, community, and neighborhood. Voting instills a sense of responsibility and connects people to the process of governing.

However, as a result of our tepid voter turnout (between 43 and 50 percent; in most European nations voter rates are higher than 70 percent), we have shown special interests and the politicians under their control that we don't care about who gets elected, or what the government actually does once it is selected.[26] We have shown the "powers-that-be" in America that we are not interested in our civic duties. By not voting we have given those in power the green light to walk all over us. And they have.

After 60 years of relinquishing the reins of power, it's time to raise our voices in the electoral process and take back our country from business interests and their political pawns. It is time to wield the power we have as citizens in a democracy and cast our votes for change.

We have been manipulated by business interests and lied to by all levels of government, and it is time for that to stop. By playing an active role in the democratic process through voting, we the people of America can take back our country from the special interests that have destroyed our cities, eliminated our transportation options, and suppressed the possibilities for community development.

Voting is an assertion that we will no longer blindly let the system speak for us. Voting is an overt display that we will once again become empowered citizens. Voting shows that we want our country to meet our needs, not just the needs of major business interests. Let's use the power given to us as citizens of a democracy. Let's vote to create a better America.

CHAPTER SEVEN

A Vision for a Better Future

If you want the future to be different from the past,
be aware. Study the past, find its causes, and bring
different causes to bear.

S MALL-SCALE INITIATIVES ARE UNDERWAY that are helping to stop
sprawl and re-establish genuine American communities by
managing growth, preserving historic neighborhoods, creating new urban centers, introducing more transportation
options, and saving farmland. Despite the tens of billions of dollars being thrown into the money pit called Iraq, Congress is also
passing bills that attempt to enhance the livability of cities and
improve public transportation. In conjunction, a diverse group of
independent organizations and government agencies that had
previously ignored sprawl — Sierra Club, American Farmland
Trust, Brookings Institution, Worldwatch Institute, Environmental
Protection Agency, and Department of Housing and Urban
Development — are now realizing that sprawl is one of the key
issues affecting America today. The National Trust for Historic
Preservation (NTHP) has recently put an entire state on its endan-
gered list — a spot usually reserved for individual buildings or

small town main streets — warning that if big box stores continue to be built in Vermont, the bucolic small towns for which the state is prized will quickly disappear.

Another NTHP initiative is their partnership with the Ad Council to create public service announcements extolling the virtues of preserving buildings, neighborhoods, and communities. Begun in late 2002, these ads are reaching Americans via radio, television, newspapers and magazines. The announcements contain playful yet poignant messages that pit positive memories of the past against the harsh reality of sprawl's impact. In one radio spot, we hear the voice of a woman recalling her marriage at a "little Presbyterian ..." and her attempt to say "church" is drowned out by another voice saying "convenience store." In a television commercial, a couple returns to the church where they were married, only to discover it has been replaced by a gas station. A voice over says, "When your children ask where you got married, will you have to say, 'Over there, by the unleaded?'"[1]

These ads, $30 million worth, will run for three years, and are a prime indicator to me that our nation is finally waking up to the harmful impact of its alienating physical landscape. Why? Because the Ad Council is the mouthpiece for the business community, and through these ads they are planting a seed in the minds of Americans that something needs to be done about sprawl. And when business wants something done in America, it usually happens. These ads are in the vanguard of a broad-based cultural change. These new media messages are the beginning of a cultural re-education program designed to convince Americans that the destruction of their urban areas, whether in small towns or city neighborhoods, should no longer be tolerated.

Ironically, these ads are reminiscent of past public relations campaigns, many also initiated by the Ad Council, which back in the 1940s and 50s convinced people to leave established urban communities, move out to suburban sprawl, and become dependent on their automobiles. The current round of ads reverses the cultural programming that the previous ads promoted.

Each year America gets closer to being livable again, but there is still a long way to go before our urban areas can be mentioned in the same positive breath as those in Europe, Australia, or Canada. Even some politicians — those individuals most loath to confess error — are jumping on the bandwagon and admitting that past urban development decisions desperately need to be rectified.

To get to where there are more than just isolated pockets of community life in America, we will need to change the cultural focus we have held for almost 60 years, and commit ourselves, at all levels of society, to improving the urban landscape. Isolated economic investment in small projects is not enough; we must all make an intellectual and spiritual commitment to creating livable places. To get this country back on the path to community again, we need to follow a new vision.

The Way America Can Be

This new vision for America offers the opportunity for more fulfilling lives and more enriching social interactions. In this vision I see tree-lined streets filled with mixed-income housing located within walking distance of the main streets of small towns, connected to one another by viable and extensive mass transit. In these places, property values will not be undermined by the proximity of different housing types, because individual homes will be part of the overall community again and not just an isolated investment commodity. As it was before World War II, the whole will again be greater than the sum of its parts.

To ensure the success of these new American neighborhoods, our entire urban landscape will maintain high standards of livability in the form of easy access to shops, recreation facilities, and public space, as well as other aspects of a healthy community. The sidewalk will be restored as the glue that holds a neighborhood together. The open, public, noncommercial spaces planned into our communities will function as outdoor "living rooms," where members of the community can connect with one another. Young and old alike will cross the generation gap and be revitalized through daily encounters. Neighbors will get to know one another, and local shopkeepers will help to develop the long-lasting, cohesive embrace of community. People will start to emerge from in front of their plug-in drugs — the television, computer, Internet, and video games — and become part of each other's lives again.

Community rebirth will not only occur with new developments in the far-flung suburbs. It will also take place in existing urban areas. The restoration of older buildings and neighborhoods will help to revive blighted or underserved locations. With more people living in renovated buildings, walking the streets, shopping at local stores, and interacting with each other, a community-oriented way of life will return. These cohesive neighborhoods will once again be safe and secure, because concerned and active citizens are the best watchdogs.

The main problem we have been facing in America for the past 50-plus years has not been growth; it has been unplanned growth. In another three decades America will have absorbed at least another 60 million more immigrants. We will need healthy and safe places to house these people. It is time to use our immense resources of capital, knowledge, and technology to modify the spaces we currently have and to create modern and livable urban environments where individuals and organizations can develop into cohesive and healthy communities.

In these communities, I see young and old interacting on a daily basis in the grand spectacle of life. Senior citizens will not be shoved aside into retirement homes, parents and families will not be isolated in their suburban fortresses, and the process of raising a child will be shared by the entire community. I envision children playing in safe environs, under the watchful attention of the whole neighborhood, after they leave school and before they wander home for an afternoon snack. I see working parents returning home from the day's labor, not always isolated in automobiles, but instead walking from the bus or trolley stop, greeting neighbors, or stopping to chat with the local baker as they pick up some fresh bread for the evening meal.

I see some parents leaning out their windows, others on their porches, directly on or near the central square, chatting with passersby, and calling to their children to come home for dinner. I can hear some families' distinct dinner bells ringing throughout the community, summoning members home for the evening repast, the smells of diverse cuisine filling the night air. After the meal, entire families will gather with friends and other members of their community at a local café or central public space to wind down for the evening and just "be" with each other.

With small local shops, farmer's markets, restaurants, cafés, coffee bars, and public spaces all within walking distance, people will begin to forsake the lure of the fantasy world of the media and get out of their homes to enjoy the company of other people. Watching less television will allow people to create their own lives and identities through community interaction instead of being sucked into the lifestyles of fashion and popular culture that advertising and the mass media promote. In the America I envision, people will be part of a cohesive, nurturing community and will not have to buy their identities, sense of belonging, or self-worth at the mall. In this vision, I see genuine American communities becoming the norm again, not the rarity that they are today.

Our journey toward community rebirth will not be a short or easy one, but it is time for us to start recreating a functioning society in America. Change is already in the air. Let's build on it. We have the strength, energy, and commitment to succeed. There is no better time than now, and no better people than us to take the first steps toward a sustainable, livable, and safe future.

In 1960, inspired by John F. Kennedy, our society committed itself to putting a man on the moon by the end of that decade. We succeeded. We have the intellectual capacity, the economic vitality, and the collective will to conquer any problem. When we put our minds to something, we get it done. Let's commit ourselves to something that will benefit more people than placing a robot on Mars. Let's stop wasting our intellectual property on finding new and better ways to make dough stay crisp when cooked in a microwave. Let's put our vast resources to good use and start making America livable again by building places where communities can form. Let's not confine another generation to the dual wastelands of sprawl and urban blight, and the fear, alienation, and isolation they breed.

As Confucius so wisely said many years ago, "A thousand-mile journey begins with one step." Who's ready to go for a walk?

How Sprawl Came to Be

> The government of cities is the one conspicuous
> failure of the United States.
>> — James Bryce

I'VE PLACED THIS SECTION ON THE HISTORY OF SPRAWL in an appendix not because it is less significant than the rest of the book, but so that its detail would not distract the reader from the book's main thrust: explaining suburbia's impact on American society, while offering practical solutions to help alleviate the isolation, alienation, and fear of living in the wasteland that is sprawl.

Clearly, we still have much to learn about organizing and managing the places where we live. Only by becoming aware of the mistakes we have made and continue to make as a nation, can we lay a firm foundation of understanding to ensure that we do not make similar mistakes in the future.

Chronicled below are the six major events, or series of events, that precipitated the emergence of sprawl, our addiction to the automobile, and the destruction of our communities. This is not a comprehensive historical study, though the research it is based on is. Instead, I have presented a distillation, a concise foundation from which to better understand why the American urban landscape is the way it is today. Each issue is presented separately, although all are interconnected.

US Government Support of Road over Rail

The railroad industry, almost since its inception, has had an adversarial relationship with the US government. These companies got immensely powerful so fast that the fledgling federal government could not control them. Instead of trying to rein them in, the government chose instead to support another form of transport — roads and the vehicles that use them — to combat the railroads' power. We're stuck with this narrowly focused, misguided legacy today.

To set the scene, let's briefly go back to an age before railroads, prior to 1850. Early American cities tended to grow as coherent forms, each with a different shape based on geography, but with a well-defined city center. Defense requirements, coupled with the need for access to waterways, tended to keep these cities tight and focused. Similarly, in the Spanish-American West, the pueblo, presidio-fort, and mission gave coherent form to Santa Fe, San Diego, Monterey, San Francisco, San Antonio, and many other settlements.[1]

Early on, a harbor or river was the central focus for cities and towns. As the nation grew and people moved westward, the railway depot, a kind of inland harbor, became the focal point. But unlike in Europe, where the railroads connected already existing towns, in America the railroads themselves helped determine where towns would be established. This ability to form and transform our nation was one manifestation of the immense power these corporate entities wielded in the mid- to late-19th century.

When Railroads Ran the Country

Railroads offered jobs to the average person, markets for growing businesses, and huge profits to shareholders. During the pre-highway era, the vast majority of marketable goods — whether steel, lumber, coal, or grain — was transported by rail. The rest were shipped along the nation's rivers and coastlines. This transportation dominance generated immense profits. Individual railroads became economic powerhouses; collectively, they were a juggernaut with enormous influence. Without the existence of strong local, state, or even federal government, the railroads, quite literally, began to run the country.

All over America their economic power allowed the railroads to put competing steamship and canal companies out of business, eliminating the only other large-scale transportation alternatives that existed. In doing so, the railroads became America's first monopoly.

This monopoly position allowed railroads to influence government officials on a dramatic scale. One example of this, by no means isolated, was the Santa Fe Railroad. During each session of government, the Santa Fe Railroad would dole out between $500 and $2,000 to each legislative leader in the jurisdictions its tracks passed through. Since these legislators earned only $3 a day, or about $600 a year, they were very susceptible to the influence of this railroad money.[2] The power of the railroad owners, who had become known as "robber barons," was so absolute that they tended to view public officeholders as field agents briefly entrusted with the management of the government for the sole purpose of assisting railroad interests.

Besides controlling governments, railroads also determined which cities and towns would survive in America's west. It was obvious to any aware civic leader that if he wanted his town to succeed, it needed to have a railway depot. Consequently, town leaders went to virtually any length to ensure that their town received a stop along the rail line. As Stephen Goddard describes in his book *Getting There*, "Railroad promoters could often dictate their price for steering tracks into town. When they called on the leaders of the fledgling town of Booneville, Iowa — demanding $10,000, and 20 acres of town land before bringing their rails in — townspeople scurried to raise all but $1,200, for which they agreed to sign a note."[3] As it turned out, this was unacceptable to the railroad promoters, and they routed the line through a more cooperative town. Today, you will search in vain for a town called Booneville in Iowa.

Besides establishing where Americans would live, the railroads also decided what got shipped, when, where, and for how much, effectively controlling the entire economy while charging exorbitant shipping rates to maximize their profits.

This economic control wreaked havoc on the profitability of small businesses and farmers who were dependent upon the rails to transport their goods. Finally fed up with the situation, in 1887 the Interstate Commerce Commission (ICC), a newly created arm of the federal government, attempted to regulate the railroad industry for the benefit of the nation.

In 1889, to combat the encroaching control of the ICC, the railroad barons met to formalize the collaboration that would forever turn the public and government against them. What became known as the Gentlemen's Agreement of 1889 was actually a rate-fixing arrangement in which two-thirds of the nation's railway companies participated. This loosely structured organization consolidated and coordinated economic control of the country.

The railroads' omnipotence may not have been challenged so soon if it weren't for a few choice words by William Vanderbilt, a powerful railroad baron, that were quoted in the *Chicago Daily News*. When asked whether his company would be interested in sustaining a loss if it were for the public's good he replied, "The public be damned." This one statement, reprinted in papers all over the nation, galvanized public and governmental wrath against the power of the railroads. To this day, the government underfunds rail transportation, while massively subsidizing road construction and air travel.

Enforcing the Sherman Antitrust Act

When Theodore Roosevelt became president in 1901, he was in the vanguard of the popular anti-big business sentiment that permeated America. He labored to ensure that there was a countervailing force to corporate power. His initial focus was on the railroads, and he would do much to make certain that their control was reduced. However, there were other businesses in America, such as the oil industry, which had also grown large and powerful. Roosevelt's mission was to cut these business entities down to size for the benefit of the common citizen, and to guarantee that government in America could actually govern. To achieve this end, his administration launched at least forty-five antitrust actions.

In 1906, his administration passed the Hepburn Act, allowing the ICC essentially to run the railroads. This act gave the federal government the power to decide exactly what the railroads could charge for freight and passengers, and to determine where and how often the trains ran. Unfortunately, since the ICC had earlier decreed that anyone who worked for the railroads could never work for the ICC, government regulators had little idea how to manage what was then the world's most complex business enterprise.

Despite its good intentions, the Hepburn Act failed to suppress the power of the railroads. Even with the restrictions placed on them by the government, the railroads continued to expand in size and profitability, mainly because they were still the only viable inter-urban transportation and freight option in America. Ten years after the act's inception, railroads employed 1.7 million Americans, had investment capital of $21 billion,[4] and had tracks spread over 254,000 miles.[5]

Cars and Roads

Realizing that it could not regulate the railroads into cooperating, the US government started to negate their power by actively supporting road construction and the industries associated with roads. At the time, such infrastructure improvement was certainly needed. By 1910, there were 468,000 automobiles struggling through the mud or being coated with dust from unpaved city and country roads.[6] Pressure to rectify this situation pushed

Congress to enact the Federal Aid Highway Act of 1916, which launched the national highway system.

Then came the 1920s, the decade when America was at its most prosperous and community-oriented. The country was filled with a positive, can-do attitude. People still lived in close-knit communities. The economy was booming, roads were being built, cars were streaming off assembly lines, trolleys ran through every major American city and were immensely popular, passenger rail was extensive, cities were livable, and small towns flourished.

The prosperity of that decade translated into car sales. Despite the poor condition of America's dirt roads, on which cars frequently got bogged down, people were buying cars in ever increasing numbers. Powerfully influenced by automobile ads and accompanying newspaper articles extolling the virtues of cars, Americans became infatuated with the automobile, ignoring the limits of its practicality.

Richard O. Davies, author of *The Age of Asphalt,* notes: "During the 1920s more than 17 million cars, trucks, and busses were added to the nation's motor fleet and the number of miles of surfaced highways reached 407,000. In ten short years, the nation's highway system had advanced from a primitive state to that of the best in the world."[7] The Federal Aid Act of 1921 allocated a large amount of money for road construction. Throughout the decade, America's roads became better than they had ever been before. However, they were still only a spider web of paved pathways, similar to the country roads of today.

Despite all this road building and the increased sales of cars, in 1927 people still used public transport extensively. In Boston only 25 percent of commuters drove to work; in Chicago, 20 percent; and in Detroit, 18 percent.[8] Our rail and trolley networks were so extensive that people had a choice. They were not yet being forced to drive to work as most commuters are today.

With the onset of the Great Depression in 1929 and then World War II in the early 1940s, government highway programs were put on hold. Getting people fed, clothed, and sheltered took precedence over the construction of roads. Then, the manufacturing of war material pushed road building even further onto the back burner.

Even though road building had stopped, and gasoline and tire rationing were in place, by 1941 the number of registered autos reached nearly 30 million, an increase of 3 million from 1939.[9] However cars weren't Americans' first choice when it came to transportation. People still rode intra-urban trolleys and passenger rail more often than they drove their automobiles.

The End of Passenger Rail

It became apparent during World War II that America's roads were not fit for carrying large amounts of military personnel or material. Trucks laden with munitions couldn't make it to destinations on time. Soldiers on maneuvers would get stuck in muddy country lanes. Out of necessity, this situation led to a revived use of railroads, which by the end of the war efficiently and effectively moved 97 percent of wartime passengers and 90 percent of all freight.[10] At this juncture, the railroads had become part of the solution, and no longer acted as arrogant, price-gouging opportunists. Everyone was working together to win the war. Prices were fair. Rails ran everywhere. Trains were on time.

Instead of taking this new attitude and the resurgence in rail patronage as a sign that rail should be supported after the war ended, the federal government continued its adversarial relationship and moved to supplant rail with still more roads. Starting in 1946, through increasingly vigorous ICC regulations and heavier investment in roads, the government began to tighten its stranglehold on the railroads.

The prices railroads could charge became increasingly regulated. The government also required that the railroads maintain all their tracks, even the least profitable, without any government assistance. These two restrictions, more than any others, stifled the ability of the railroads to compete with the coalition of road builders, automobile manufacturers, and oil companies that the federal government supported through subsidized road building. These road subsidies amounted to 75 percent of all transportation expenditures in the postwar generation.[11] The era of railroad pre-eminence was about to end.

At the same time, profits for members of the powerful business cartel called the highway lobby (an entity covered in more detail in the "Trolley Systems Destroyed" section) had skyrocketed. All the cars, trucks, jeeps, and tanks that had been built for the war effort, as well as the oil, gasoline, and lubricants sold to run them, filled the coffers of auto and oil companies to overflowing. This money meant power in postwar America. The stage was set for the highway lobby to completely reshape America to accommodate the automobile.

After the war, passenger railways attempted to retain the premier position they had re-established during the war, despite the deck being stacked against them. But without government money to help them maintain their tracks, and as a result of increasing competition from government-sponsored road systems, passenger railroads experienced a rapid decline. Rail companies folded, reducing citizens' transportation options, and encouraging people to buy cars for use on the roads being built by the government. This pattern of narrow-mindedly excluding passenger rail from the transportation picture continues today.

Only recently has our government made a tentative commitment to passenger rail. On September 6, 2001, Congress announced the intent to support a high-speed rail bill with $71 billion. However, five days later terrorists rammed two planes into the Twin Towers in New York and another into the Pentagon, and the money from that bill never materialized. Instead of being used to fund a necessary diversification of our transportation system, the money allocated for high-speed passenger rail went instead to buttress the airline industry and fund the wars in Afghanistan and Iraq.

Frank Lloyd Wright, Robert Moses, and FDR

A pivotal moment in the establishment of sprawl occurred when President Franklin Delano Roosevelt became enamored of Frank Lloyd Wright's vision for America's urban spaces. Though a brilliant architect of individual buildings, Wright left much to be desired in terms of his overall urban vision. World-renowned urban planner Lewis Mumford described Wright as being "without any disturbing afterthoughts about the relation of his architectural fantasies to the needs and functions they served, or the conditions of the climate and weather they had to meet, or their responsibility to the neighborhood or community."[12] Despite his limitations as an urban planner, Wright's misguided ideas were the ones our government chose as its model.

When Roosevelt became president on March 4, 1933, he ushered in a new way of dealing with the Great Depression. His grand plan for economic recovery consisted of a variety of spending initiatives led by the government, with civilian organizations coordinating complementary efforts. FDR was looking for solutions to problems that had never before existed, and in doing so he experimented with many different untested methods. Some of them worked, others did not. Regrettably, one idea FDR latched onto was Wright's vision of creating a suburban nation where everyone drove an automobile. Such a landscape, Wright proposed, while being modern and (in his mind) efficient, would also create jobs through the construction of automobiles, new homes, and roads.

The suburban pipe dream that Wright sold FDR was called Broadacre City, a place with houses on one-acre lots and segregated land use, where everyone needed a car. It was an idealistic array of uncommon tidiness and order that looked good on an architect's drawing board but did not work in reality.

Along with Wright, the other individual who had a profound impact on FDR's urban planning initiatives was Robert Moses, a man dubbed by *The Atlantic Monthly* as "The Godfather of Sprawl," whose development projects have left scars all over New York State. Moses has been credited with doing as much to promote the use of the automobile as Henry Ford. Car lovers are forever in his debt, but supporters of public transportation and livable communities may never forgive him.

When Robert Moses came to power in 1934, first as head of the Parks Commissions of New York and Long Island, and eventually as New York City Parks Commissioner and head of the Triborough Bridge and Tunnel Authority, New York's mass transit system was the best in the developed world. When he fell from power in 1968, it was among the worst.[13] During his tenure managing New York State's public works, more than 600 miles of expressways were built around New York City, but not a single mile of subway was initiated. At the same time, he effectively prohibited buses from using the parkways he built, because the overpasses were constructed so low that buses could not drive under them. Public transportation was not part of Moses's mission. His focus was to promote individual automobile usage, and he did it with a vengeance, paving the way for the country as we know it: full of unsafe cities and wastelands of sprawl.

Ignored in FDR's rush to embrace the vision offered by Wright and Moses, was the already successful Garden City model for town planning that had been flourishing all over the country for decades. Initially promoted by Ebenezer Howard, this popular Garden City approach built small towns on a human scale, places that were walkable and connected to one another by public transportation. Prior to FDR, the Garden City model was America's preferred method for the planning and development of suburbia. After FDR's administration, such community-oriented places would no longer be built.

Early Suburban Development – Healthy Communities

To better conceptualize what Frank Lloyd Wright and Robert Moses helped destroy, we need to understand that before the ideas of those two individuals became pre-eminent, American cities and suburbs were profoundly livable. They were not perfect by any stretch of the imagination, but they were much better than the inner-city urban blight, downtown office ghettoes, and alienating suburban sprawl that exist today.

American cities were compact grids of close-knit, community-oriented neighborhoods. To be sure, some early American city neighborhoods were troubled by crime, overcrowding, and lack of sanitation. However, American cities were also places where communities flourished, where people possessed a sense of pride rooted in a sense of place.[14]

The growth in our cities' population created a need for more housing and better public transportation. About the time of the Civil War, omnibuses called "streetcars" emerged that were drawn by horses, first on the streets themselves, then eventually along rails. Early streetcar stops were located along existing urban cores where stores, homes, and apartments were already located. As their tracks extended farther out, streetcar stops became the central cores around which small town-style main streets and neighborhoods began to emerge where none had been before.

Soon to be called "streetcar suburbs," these bucolic settings started sprouting dramatically in the 1880s to ease the congestion in cities, and to cater to America's emerging middle class. Wherever a trolley stop was placed, urban cores would also be developed, complete with all the amenities of living and the accompanying sense of community.

As late as 1850 the city of Boston, for example, was still a compact pedestrian city with a mere three-mile radius. But by 1900 the city had become an amalgamation of villages, surrounded by suburbs served by streetcars extending out to a ten-mile radius.

Near the end of the nineteenth century, with the electrification of streetcars, now called trolleys, cities all over America extended their limits. These electric trolley lines were built outward from the central cores of established cities and, even as they diffused the population, they continued to nourish the old city centers while creating smaller cores of livability on the outskirts.

Whether railroad or streetcar suburb, early American suburban developments had a central focus. These small towns were constructed around public transportation stops. They were not haphazardly thrown up all over the landscape, as with the sprawled development inspired by Frank Lloyd Wright and Robert Moses.

Garden City Suburbs

The Garden City model promoted by English planner Ebenezer Howard adhered to successful Old World patterns of urban development. Strongly influenced by the attempts of powerful industrialists, such as W.H. Lever and George Cadbury, to create healthy, well-planned model communities to house their workers, in 1898 Howard put a synthesis of these ideas into a published work, *Garden Cities of Tomorrow.* It soon became the bible for suburban town planning in America. The Garden City model for urban development created just the kinds of places that helped to make life livable, fulfilling and meaningful. Figures A.1 and A.2 show prime examples of small town suburban developments patterned on the Garden City model: the types of places that were built in America prior to World War II. (See "Introduction: Overview" for more information on Garden City suburbs.)

Greenbelt Towns

Unfortunately, once the Garden City model was superseded by the ideas of Frank Lloyd Wright and Robert Moses, America would never be the same. Wright's Broadacre concept of dispersed housing came into reality with the Greenbelt Town Program, a series of towns built and planned by the US government during the New Deal as public housing projects for the middle class.

Initially based on the Garden City model, Greenbelt towns eventually metastasized into something else entirely. In the beginning, Rexford Tugwell, FDR's Director of the Resettlement Administration, the agency responsible for developing the Greenbelt

Figure A.1

INDIAN HEAD GOVERNMENT HOUSING PROJECT, MARYLAND, 1920s

Courtesy of the Frances Loeb Library, Harvard Design School

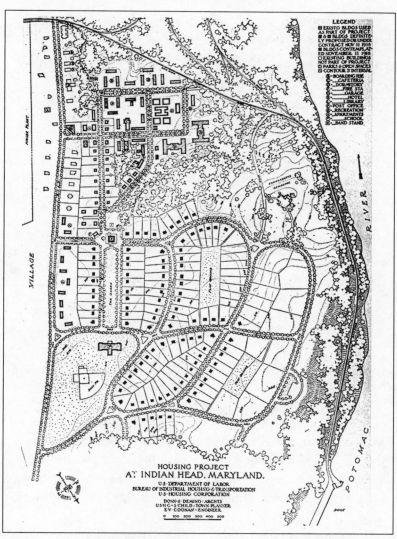

An example of a successful Garden City suburban development in the 1920s. Please note the legend, which indicates the public facilities incorporated into this plan. Please also note the mixed-use facilities and the different housing types, all of which helped to give this suburban development a small-town atmosphere.

Figure A.2
MARE ISLAND GOVERNMENT HOUSING PROJECT, CALIFORNIA, 1915

Courtesy of the Frances Loeb Library, Harvard Design School

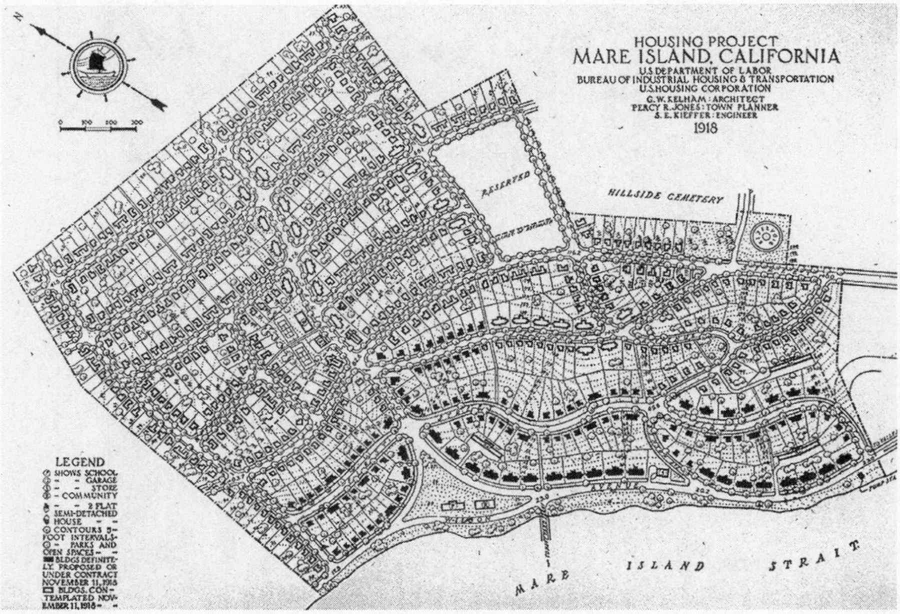

Another example of a successful Garden City suburban development model. Note the legend, which indicates the public facilities and the commercial property incorporated into this plan, as well as the different housing types.

towns, urged the establishment of several thousand Garden City suburbs. The architects and planners working for this agency, among the most celebrated in their professions, were committed to building complete communities based on Ebenezer Howard's ideas.

However, this philosophy of village style housing connected by public transport went contrary to what the highway lobby wanted (more on them in the next section). As a result, the proven development pattern of Garden City suburbs was discarded.

Of the three thousand Greenbelt towns Tugwell envisioned, only three ended up being funded by Congress.[15] And they were so spread out that they were more like Wright's Broadacre concept. (See Figure A.3) They were the beginnings of sprawl.

To be fair, Greenbelt towns did incorporate many of the functions of life into one development. But unlike the Garden

Figure A.3

GREENBELT PLAN, MARYLAND

Courtesy of the Frances Loeb Library, Harvard Design School

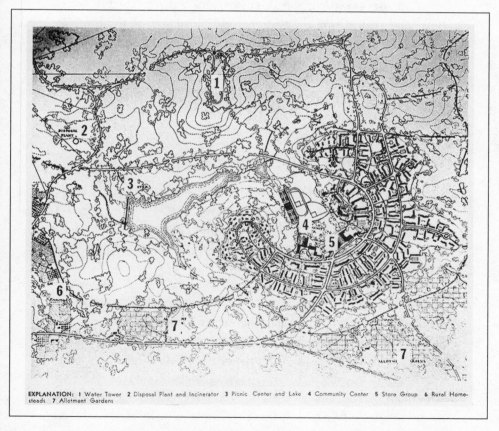

EXPLANATION: 1 Water Tower 2 Disposal Plant and Incinerator 3 Picnic Center and Lake 4 Community Center 5 Store Group 6 Rural Homesteads 7 Allotment Gardens

An example of a government sponsored project to create a suburb centered around the use of automobiles. Note how the functions of life are more spread out than in Garden City suburbs.

City suburbs, in Greenbelt towns the central core of shops, restaurants, and other amenities were not within walking distance of most homes, which made it necessary to own a car to get around.

Despite its flaws, if the Greenbelt-style of urban development had been continued by the federal government, American suburbs would not be the wastelands they are today. However, with the onset of World War II, these and all other government-sponsored housing programs were put on hold. The government's active role in the formation of a national urban plan ended with the development of the three isolated Greenbelt towns.

After the war, the government became a disengaged nonparticipant, bequeathing the responsibility for creating the foundation upon which our society was to be built — its urban places — to private real estate speculators. Without government directing the process of urban planning, real estate companies began to build wherever there was land, regardless of the impact on society or communities.

Trolley Systems Destroyed

The trolley was as American an invention as hamburgers, apple pie, and baseball. And it was just as popular. However, this did not help American trolley systems from being completely eradicated all over the country. The trolley's demise was a major contributing factor to the spread of sprawl.

Soon after Frank J. Sprague used electricity to power the Union Passenger horsecars in Richmond, Virginia, in 1887, other streetcar entrepreneurs quickly converted to electricity since it slashed operating costs and could move vehicles faster, further, and more efficiently.[16] By the turn of the century electric streetcars, now known as trolleys, were a well-integrated facet of American life. Because of their convenience, comfort, ease of use, safety, availability, and low cost, trolleys were universally loved and patronized all over America. They transported people everywhere they needed or wanted to go.

Few inventions had ever been embraced more quickly by more people than the electric streetcar. By 1902, a federal census showed that electric trolley systems carried over five billion people a year, were capitalized with over $2 billion, and had 22,000 miles of track in place.[17] In 1912, every person who lived in a city of 100,000 or more rode public transport an average of 252 times per year.[18] However, as the prices of automobiles fell within reach of the average worker, cars started to muscle in on the trolley's popularity. In 1921 only nine million automobiles were registered in the US. By 1924, as prices fell, that number rose to 16 million.[19] Because of increased auto usage, by 1926 trolleys had reached their peak with 17.2 billion riders. By 1930 trolley ridership had fallen to 15.6 billion.[20]

While private automobiles began to flourish because taxpayers' money was being used to build roads, mass transportation began to flounder because the government chose to designate streetcar companies as private industries, not public transportation. Building roads for automobiles was considered a public service, even a necessity, while mass transit, something that billions of people used each year, was not. As a result of this bias, as early as 1910 American urban transit, which was once the envy of the world, was slowly being overtaken in size and usage by Europe.[21]

At first many people who owned cars still rode the electric trolley to work, then used their cars on weekends. People had a variety of transportation options, as is the case in Europe today. But oil and automobile companies, as well as those in the business of building roads, did not want to share any of the transportation pie.

Battle Between Trolley and Car

The battle between the trolley and the car had its roots in the 1880s — before the car was invented or the internal combustion engine was in commercial use — when the main product of oil companies was kerosene for lamps. Kerosene dramatically changed American life, lighting homes, offices, and factories, which made for longer work days, and more enjoyable family life.

Then, in 1882, standing in the office of his banker, J.P. Morgan, Thomas Edison threw a switch to start an electric generating plant. Because of electricity's cleanliness, safety, and efficiency, in a few years it almost completely supplanted kerosene for lighting. Electrification quickly forced the oil industry to scramble to find new markets for its products.

"Yet as one market was slipping away, another was opening — that of the 'horseless carriage,' otherwise known as the automobile. Some of these vehicles were powered by the internal combustion engine, which harnessed a channeled explosion of gasoline for propulsion."[22] During these initial formative years in the late 1890s and early 1900s, steam and electricity power were also tested for use with cars. By 1905, however, gasoline-powered engines had defeated steam and electricity as the most efficient means of automobile locomotion. With the internal combustion engine, oil companies soon had a potentially huge market for a new product — gasoline. Now all they had to do was convince people to buy vehicles that used a gasoline-fueled engine. That wasn't as easy as you would imagine. Trolleys still existed and millions of Americans were riding them. People did not need cars to get around as they do today. They had real choices. Because of this, oil and automobile companies realized that the only way to create enough demand for gasoline was to get people off public transportation and into cars.

The oil companies and fledgling automobile businesses tried everything to get Americans to buy cars. They lowered prices, offered easy credit, kept gas prices low, and created enticing ads. Autos were actually more affordable back in the 1920s than they are now. Because people weren't buying enough cars, the oil companies and other members of the corporate cartel and lobbying group called the highway lobby — tire manufacturers, parts suppliers, service station owners, road builders, land developers, and bankers — decided to change their line of attack. Instead of enticing riders away from the trolleys, they chose to eliminate the electric trolleys altogether. A brilliant tactical ploy, except for one small consideration: it was illegal under the Sherman Antitrust Act.

The key members of the highway lobby — General Motors, Standard Oil, Firestone Tire and Rubber, Greyhound Bus Lines, and a number of other companies — knew that viable public transportation had to be severely curtailed if they were going to sell all the oil, gas, and automobiles they intended to. This would involve getting American families to own two, if not three, cars. This corporate strategy was first voiced by automobile manufacturers in 1929.[23] To reach this goal, trolley systems had to be eliminated.

The highway lobby's plan for automobile dominance began to take coherent shape in the 1930s when General Motors approached the electric utility companies, which owned most of the urban trolley lines, and offered to buy their electric streetcar lines.[24] The electric utility companies wouldn't sell, and for good reason. Trolleys were an ideal conduit through which they were able to sell their main product, electricity.

Undeterred, the highway lobby decided to outflank their rivals by influencing Congress to make it illegal for utility companies to own trolley lines. In the end, through an intense lobbying effort, the Wheeler-Rayburn Act of 1935 was passed, requiring that utility companies divest themselves of businesses that did not specifically generate electricity.[25] Though the trolleys were for sale on the open market, it would be against the law for automobile companies or oil companies to buy them up and shut them down. The Sherman Antitrust Act specifically prohibited the inhibition of trade by a direct competitor. But that is exactly what the highway lobby was about to do.

To hide their involvement, the automobile and oil companies created a series of holding companies with the specific mission of buying up public trolley systems and shutting them down. In the 1930s and 40s they created Pacific City Lines (PCL) and National City Lines (NCL) for the sole task of eliminating the most extensive and popular public transportation system America had ever known.

Their mandate was simple: go into a city, buy up the trolley company, tear up its tracks, scrap the trolley cars, and shut the company down. The day NCL or PCL agreed to buy a trolley system, the process of systematic destruction was set in motion. Fares were increased, routes were canceled, trolleys cars were taken out of service, schedules were reduced, salaries of workers were cut, and maintenance was neglected. Over time, passengers were literally forced off the trolleys, and soon the last trolley disappeared along with its tracks.[26]

Trolleys to Buses to Cars

In the pursuit of increased profits, the highway lobby ended up illicitly eliminating well-loved and necessary trolley systems in more than 150 cities all over the country.

In their places, the highway lobby deployed a skeleton fleet of buses, a token gesture at continuing viable public transit. However, "riders were not enthusiastic about buses, which were more foul smelling, noisier, less comfortable, and slower than rail transit."[27] Buses also could not carry as many passengers per trip as rail transit, causing uncomfortable crowding. The purposeful inadequacy of buses discouraged people from using public transportation altogether, prompting them to buy cars — exactly what the highway lobby had intended.

The *coup de grace* was in Los Angeles. It is difficult to imagine that the traffic-congested city of Los Angeles once had the most extensive mass transit rail system in the world, but it did. You could go virtually anywhere in and around LA on fast, efficient, and inexpensive trolleys. More than 2,700 trains a day left from the center of LA to outlying stations like Redlands, Corona, Santa Monica, Redondo Beach, and Balboa (see Figure 1.1 in Chapter 1).[28] But that system, with 1,164 miles of inter- and intra-urban electric trolley track was unceremoniously destroyed.[29]

It was well known then, and is still true today, that highway travel is wasteful and expensive. A single lane of highway, with cars carrying an average of 1.1 people (the national average) accommodates fewer than 5,000 people an hour. A railway car moves 50,000 passengers in the same hour, with less pollution and less congestion.[30] Automobiles are ten times less efficient than railways and more destructive socially and environmentally. But this reality did not stop the government from supporting roads over rail.

Up until the end of World War II, there were still bucolic small towns outside of every American city, connected to the city center by extensive rail transport. "At the end of the war, the suburbs were still largely rural. When you reached the city limits you often came upon a landscape of pastureland, cornfields, gardens, and forests," notes Marty Jezer in his book *The Dark Ages: Life in the United States 1945-1960*.[31]

But after 1945, in only ten short years, our country would be changed completely. While our standard of living was increasing, our quality of life, sense of community, connection to place, and sense of belonging were being destroyed. After 1945 America would rapidly be turned into a wasteland of sprawl.

Slap on the Wrist for the Highway Lobby

After the war, the highway lobby continued its campaign to buy up trolley companies and put them out of business. Now, however, this was no longer occurring behind the cover of a world war, and citizens began to complain about the loss of their trolley systems. Transportation experts presented detailed studies showing local governments that rail transit helps prevent congestion on the roads, provides more efficient use of space, offers faster service, and carries more passengers than buses. But citizens and experts alike were ignored, and the destruction of trolley and rail transport continued.

By 1955, the majority of American cities had been successfully motorized, and electric trolleys were a thing of the past. Corporate greed and disregard for the public good pushed the trolley into extinction. In only one decade, 1945 to 1955, a popular and efficient mode of transportation that had been a major part of the American way of life since the end of the nineteenth century was gone. However, the highway lobby wasn't stopping there.

Veterans' Loans and the FHA

Besides subjecting our society to a crudely over-simplified and inefficient method of mono-transportation — a regression from the complex many-faceted transportation system we once boasted — the highway lobby, and their partners in the federal government, wanted to change our entire urban landscape as well. This urban alteration effort was initiated first with the Federal Housing Administration (FHA), and then with the GI Bill.

Two days after D-Day, Congress passed the Servicemen's Readjustment Act of 1944 (more familiarly known as the GI Bill), which created the Veteran's Administration (VA) and the VA Loan Guaranty Program. This program offered returning veterans easy access to credit for education, family support, and housing, all at low four percent rates of interest. Much of this money ended up being used to buy homes. However, in order to this, there was one small string attached.

Rules for VA housing loans were similar to those that existed for FHA loans at the time. Both stipulated that loans could only be used on newly built, single-family, detached homes. The FHA had "set up minimum requirements for lot size, setback from the street, separation from adjacent structures, and even the width of the house itself."[32] VA loans followed the same restrictions. Therefore, if veterans wanted to buy an existing home or an apartment in the city or a streetcar suburb, they could not do it using a low-interest VA loan. In order to reap the rewards that Uncle Sam was offering them, veterans were forced to buy new houses outside of established urban areas. This precipitated a mass exodus to the distant suburbs, places that had absolutely no amenities save for newly erected cookie-cutter homes.

The emerging suburbs were nothing like those which were built before World War II. They were far removed from any urban core and did not have adequate access to public transportation. Buying a home using a VA loan meant buying a home in the suburbs, which also meant buying a car. Sprawl and automobile dependency had begun in earnest.

From 1944 to 1952, VA loans were used in over four million mortgages, helping to fuel the biggest building boom in US history. From 1950 to 1960 almost half of all housing was built using either FHA or VA financing. The $119 billion that the FHA issued in mortgage insurance in the first four decades of its operation was used mainly to build suburban sprawl.[33]

VA and FHA discriminatory lending practices that blacklisted areas based on geographic location and which required specific types of housing to be built, were significant reasons for the proliferation of sprawled suburbs. One prominent developer, the Levitt family of Long Island, benefited greatly from these loans. They began their postwar building boom with the construction of Levittown, NY, in 1946. Built on 4,000 acres of former potato farms on Long Island, it was the largest private housing project in US history. In the first weekend of sales, over 300 homes were sold at prices ranging from $7,990 to $9,500. Upon completion it included more than 17,000 4-room Cape Cod-style cottages and 70,000 residents.

After the war, development companies such as the Levitts focused only on building residential property. There were no VA or FHA loans to build small town main streets, schools, libraries, public squares, or any other type of mixed-use development where communities could form. The growth of sprawl was rapid. In 1955 alone, nearly 8 million new cars were sold, a record at the time, and more than 1.6 million new housing starts, the vast majority of which were in the suburbs.[34]

Commercial Lenders Follow Suit
Once the government had established the rules for FHA and VA loans, commercial lenders quickly altered their policies as well.

Mortgage lending rules were changed to accommodate suburban but not urban housing.[35] All over the country, entire city neighborhoods were redlined, banning them from receiving loans for residential and commercial development. It became almost impossible for people living in cities to get loans for home improvements.

The only neighborhoods that survived despite the redlining were close-knit ethnic enclaves, such as the North End in Boston and Greenwich Village in New York City. In these locations residents bypassed the official banking system, pooled their own money in a manner similar to the housing cooperatives that flourished in the 18th and 19th centuries, and implemented rehabilitation work on their own. Today, the North End and Greenwich Village are two of the most frequently visited American urban neighborhoods because of the charm and livability they exude. Other, less cohesive neighborhoods not saved by their residents were left to rot or were bulldozed. Regrettably, many neighborhoods that were razed all over America would be considered national treasures today.

Urban "Renewal"

Despite the increasing number of people living in the newly built suburbs who needed cars to get around, the highway lobby was still not satisfied with automobile sales and gasoline consumption. In the 1950s, many Americans continued to reside and work in cities, because our cities were still safe and livable. These city folk did not need cars, a situation that the highway lobby found unacceptable. So once again the highway lobby turned to the US Congress for help. Yet another law was going to be passed to further support suburbanization and automobile dependency.

From the mid 1950s through the 1960s, with a movement ironically called "urban renewal," our government implemented unproven urban and transportation schemes that turned our cities into dehumanizing wastelands. At the end of this era the greater part of every American city would be unrecognizable as viable habitat.

The process of conscious and committed urban destruction started with the 1949 Federal Housing Act. This bill initiated urban renewal by calling for "a decent home and a suitable housing environment for every American family" and mandated the use of federal funds for the construction of more than 800,000 units of public housing.[36] That was the theory. In reality, urban renewal resulted in the obliteration of vital city neighborhoods, and turned hundreds of thousands of Americans into refugees in their own country.

Promoted as a way to improve the country, in reality urban renewal was a way for prime urban residential neighborhoods to be condemned and converted into high-priced commercial real estate. Downtown business interests and local real estate developers, with the willing assistance of government at every level, were about to alter the fabric of America society so they could make lots and lots of money. The casualties were irreplaceable. Beautiful old downtown buildings, architectural gems, were bulldozed to make way for more modern and profitable structures. Other victims were the inner-city communities of people who lived in vibrant, safe and cohesive neighborhoods.

This process of urban destruction got underway with vigor in 1954 when several changes were made to the 1949 Housing Act, making it more appealing to real estate interests. With the recommendation of the 1953 Presidential Commission on Urban Renewal and Housing, the 1949 bill was altered to allow commercial buildings to replace homes. The era of downtown office desolation, what I call "office ghettos" throughout this book, had begun.

Government and Business Collude

The 1953 presidential commission also advocated the formation of a national group called ACTION (American Council to Improve Our Neighborhoods), propaganda-speak to hide the group's true intent. The organization's role was to promote urban destruction nationwide, which it did with enthusiasm.

The first group to get involved was the Ad Council, a mouthpiece for corporate policies that, to this day, continues to present itself as the paragon of objectivity. It announced a new national advertising campaign called "Action on Slums." Simultaneously, various real estate and home-building associations began conducting their own advertising campaigns under such slogans as "Build America Better," "New Face for America," and "Better America, Inc."

These advertising efforts were combined with a concerted publicity campaign of magazine and newspaper articles promoting urban renewal and the suburban way of life. This powerful one-two punch of ads and articles helped to convince many more Americans to leave cities and move to the suburbs.

Livable neighborhoods and vibrant communities were replaced by office buildings. As rates for commercial property are generally much higher than rates for residential, this allowed already wealthy land owners to charge more for their existing real estate. Profit once again won out over human values.

All these steps occurred in concert: federal bills were passed, presidential commissions were created, federal bills were altered, task forces were established, ad campaigns were launched, and promotional efforts were initiated. This coordination indicated a clear pattern of collusion among different industries, as well as between large corporate interests and government. In the end, the needs of the American people were left out in the cold.

City Neighborhoods Destroyed

Urban renewal was designed to eradicate "slums" in the inner city, or so the ad campaigns claimed. In reality, viable city neighborhoods were destroyed all over America — places that would be described today as the perfect locations in which to live and raise a family. In many cases, neighborhoods were designated as slums based solely on statistical criteria — population density and the age of the buildings — rather than on whether they were actually problematic places to live.[37]

If these same criteria were used today, most of the best city neighborhoods in the country would have to be razed. Older structures are the ones with the most appeal; they lend

character to neighborhoods. At the same time, a dense population allows communities to form more easily, helping to sustain
small, local businesses.

The so-called "slums" flattened in the 1950s and 60s were
actually thriving communities with beautiful and structurally
sound brick and stone buildings containing shops, restaurants,
banks, offices, and homes of all kinds. It was once normal for
Americans to live in the same home, in the same neighborhood,
their entire lives. In many cases people would raise their families
in the home where they had grown up. Urban renewal completely eliminated all that.

One instance of this misguided destruction occurred in Southwest Washington, DC. This area of our nation's capital was a
thriving village-like community, filled with multi-ethnic families
— black, white, Hispanic, Catholic, Jewish, Protestant — who had
lived together in the neighborhood for generations. What the government called a slum and targeted for urban renewal, the residents
in Southwest DC called home. They appreciated the area for its
rich web of extended families, strong friendships, convenient shopping, and accessible work. This neighborhood, and others like it
in cities all over the country, were genuine communities where
people valued the place as well as the people who lived there.

In the 1950s, 20,000 residents were forced to relocate to make
way for a failed urban experiment called L'Enfant Plaza. Despite
the obvious community-oriented nature of the existing neighborhood, residents were evicted from their homes and all the
buildings were demolished to create what is still today a bland
office ghetto, devoid of any community life. This is but one
example of the wholesale slaughter of vibrant inner-city neighborhoods caused by urban "renewal."

1956 Interstate Highway Bill

Urban renewal was an immense undertaking, but it was soon to
be dwarfed by the 1956 Interstate Highway Bill. This bill initiated

the largest public works project the world had ever seen. To fully appreciate the size and scope of this $50 billion effort that created the National System of Interstate and Defense Highways (more popularly known as the Interstate Highway System), keep in mind that the entire federal budget at the time was only $71 billion.[38]

The 1956 Interstate Highway Act quite literally decimated the American landscape. Forests and fields were paved over, cities were sliced apart, neighborhoods were leveled, and the entire urban environment was ransacked, desecrated, and demolished.

The interstate highway system was an equal opportunity demolisher. All the highway builders seemed to care about was making room for their roads. The highway engineer did not hesitate to lay waste to woods, streams, parks, and human neighborhoods — all to ensure that the roads reached their destination.[39] And the American people, Congress, and every President, Republican or Democrat, since Eisenhower stepped aside to let them do it.

The 1956 Highway Bill was enacted so easily because it was an economic windfall for politicians — 90 percent of the cost of all road construction was funded by the federal government. It was like manna from heaven descending on 406 out of 435 Congressional districts.[40] Local government officials couldn't get in line fast enough to accept the highway handouts. Regardless of whether the construction would help their constituents, politicians built highways for the simple reason that it would create jobs and improve local economies, which in turn would help them get re-elected.

Road builders may have achieved stunning feats of structural engineering, but the highways they erected were a social catastrophe. Today we are left with the sad legacy of this short-sighted period in our history. Every American city now has at least one highway slicing through its heart. Looking at an atlas of the US, you cannot help but notice how our cities are scarred with highways. They may look attractive, colorful, and efficient on a map, but down on the ground highways represent abject urban destruction.

The government blatantly thrust automobile dependency on every American. Sprawl did not just happen. It was created. And the 1956 Highway Bill was the final nail in the coffin of the quality of life that comes from living in a community.

The Highway "Trust" Fund

Construction of highways ended up being like a demolition derby on amphetamines. Even after major opposition to the massive highway projects emerged, it would take decades before anyone could slow down the process, mainly due to a unique aspect of this particular bill. Through the collection of new federal taxes, the federal government was footing 90 percent of the costs associated with highway construction. These funds were collected and dispersed by a single entity, the Highway Trust Fund — an ironic name for something that ended up betraying the trust of every American.

The Highway Trust Fund collected the federal taxes on lubricating oils and gasoline, as well as any excise taxes on buses and trucks, and pooled these moneys into one big pot destined only for new highway construction. It worked like this: the Highway Trust Fund taxed citizens who bought the products of one arm of the highway lobby (oil and gas), then sent that money directly to other highway lobby members (bankers and construction contractors) to build more roads. Still other members of the lobby (auto, rubber, electronics, glass, real estate) benefited by the increased purchases of new automobiles stimulated by newer and better roads. These new cars then started the whole ball rolling again by increasing the sales of oil and gas and generating sales tax revenue. All this was done with minimal government oversight or involvement beyond the dispersal of funds. The Highway Trust Fund was almost a law unto itself.

States, counties, and municipalities bent over backwards to get this free money, allowing construction to cut through urban centers and pave over farmland. All this was done in the name of progress, jobs, and tax revenue. Few people in power seemed to care about the adverse impact these highways were having on society at large.

From 1956 to 1972, the years that the Highway Bill had the most impact, millions of people were forced out of their homes and businesses. To this day, the Highway Trust Fund is almost completely sacrosanct, with the result that vital public transportation projects such as high speed rail still remain grossly underfunded.

Public Outrage

Public forums began sprouting up in affected cities to offer a venue for citizens wanting to vent their frustration. The ever-present specter of the executioners' wrecking ball galvanized citizens to organize anti-highway demonstrations all across America during the 1960s. The people being displaced by highways were screaming for a halt to the destruction. In 1967, busloads of Bostonians came to Washington to picket Congress over a planned eight-lane highway that would cut across their city. This group, the "Save Our Cities Committee," was able to stop that specific project, but others would follow that the people could not halt.

Demonstrations and pickets sprang up all over the country to stop highway construction, but the "highwaymen" usually won these battles, because highways meant jobs, profits, dividends, bonuses, and payoffs for politicians. The politicians' hearts had been closed to the needs of the people by easily accessible and plentiful highway money. People aren't profitable; highways are.

Inner City Riots

As highway construction and urban renewal carved up healthy, livable urban neighborhoods to accommodate automobiles, millions of Americans became refugees in their own country. The most directly affected were the disenfranchised, the urban poor, who were predominantly African-American. Urban destruction played a large part in fomenting the unrest that caused inner city residents to fight back in the 1960s.

Highway construction crushed the sense of opportunity in the inner city, the hope of residents that they might be able to rise above poverty. Without the economic means to move to the suburbs, as well as being legally barred because of their race (America was still a racist apartheid system at the time), African-American sentiments began to boil over. Inner city residents' pleas to stop the destruction of their neighborhoods were ignored, so they rebelled.

It goes without saying that if inner city neighborhoods had not been destroyed, the economic base of cities would not have been lost. Safe inner-city communities would have continued to exist, and African-Americans would have continued to progress economically and socially, as they had during World War II.

Instead, highway construction set the stage for inner-city revolt, which first erupted in 1965 in the Watts section of Los Angeles. This spectacle of fiery rebellion, looting, and vandalism foreshadowed what was soon to occur all over the country. In the summer of 1967, major cities across America — Tampa, Cincinnati, Atlanta, Newark, Detroit — went up in flames.[41] Urban renewal, the destruction of neighborhoods, freeway construction, and the lack of public transportation to get to suburban jobs were all reasons given by residents for the urban riots. But no one was listening.

Just before the eruption of violence in 1968, the Kerner Commission was appointed by Congress to investigate inner-city unrest. When they released their report on March 1, 1968 one of their suggestions was for more mass transit to link city workers with employers who had moved to the suburbs. Unfortunately, that logical conclusion was ignored and is only being implemented on a small scale today, over 35 years later.

The destruction of cities by riots suited the purposes of the highway lobby perfectly. Now American cities were almost completely uninviting. As a result, many of the remaining individuals who had the economic and legal means to leave followed the herd out to suburbia and automobile ownership. Sprawl had become the only option left. Our cities were effectively left for dead.

Everything Went According to Plan

The highway lobby and the US government got exactly what they wanted — a car-centric suburban culture. By the end of the 1960s, Americans would need an automobile to go almost anywhere; and sprawl, the antithesis of livability, is now where Americans live.

It is obvious from studying our country's past that the American urban environment once was, and could still be, filled with character and charm.[42] But by placing urban development in the hands of highway engineers, real estate speculators, and zoning officials — instead of trained, objective urban planners as is the case in every other developed nation — American cities became desolate war zones and office wastelands. At the same time, our bucolic small towns, pristine farmland, and virgin countryside were converted into uncontrolled suburban sprawl.

Sprawl Raises Local Taxes

E ACH OF THESE EXAMPLES ILLUMINATES SPRAWL'S ROLE in raising local taxes. None of them is unique. You will find examples like this all over the country.

- From 1970 to 1995, Maine spent over $338 million building new schools, while the number of public school students declined by 27,000.[1] As people moved out of urban areas, schools had to be built farther and farther from existing urban developments. Every resident of Maine had to pay for these new schools, whether they used them or not.

- The cost of extending new infrastructure (e.g., roads, electricity, water lines, sewers, and schools) to new subdivisions in Oregon now averages $25,000 per home.[2] The existing taxpayers pick up this tab.

- Since 1980, the city of Fresno has doubled in size, producing $56 million in yearly revenues, but the cost of services has risen to $123 million. This figure does not include the costs associated with building roads and sewers.[3] Developers, who created the need for services by building sprawl, do not pay for the shortfall between annual revenues and the cost of services; the residents of the city of Fresno do.

- If Albuquerque, New Mexico, continues its current rate of growth, the city and surrounding Bernalillo County will have to come up with $3.2 billion to pay for the necessary roads, drainage systems, water, and sewer lines needed over the next 20 years.[4]

- Between 1970 and 1990, Minneapolis-St. Paul closed 162 functioning schools in existing areas and opened 78 brand new schools in the sprawling suburbs.[5] The costs associated with these schools — which would not have been necessary if development patterns had been better managed — are not paid for by the developers who created the need for them. Every resident of the Twin Cities paid for these new schools, even if they did not use them.

- Planners in Minneapolis-St. Paul estimate it will cost $3.1 billion for new water and sewage services alone to accommodate projected growth between now and 2020.[6] Developers will not foot this bill, taxpayers will.

- Even though Prince William County, Virginia, has the highest property tax rate in the state, providing services for new development results in a $1,688 shortfall for every new house built, because of the need for added services.[7] That shortfall is passed on to every member of the county, whether they benefit from the new development or not.

Resource List

Part One — Organizations

Listed below are a number of organizations that are active in helping to enhance the livability of neighborhoods, towns, and cities. Whether through farmland protection, rails to trails conversion, transportation initiatives, social policy development, or the application of New Urbanism practices, each of these groups is part of a growing awareness that our urban spaces hold the key to enhancing the community-oriented livability and safety of our entire nation.

American Farmland Trust

American Farmland Trust is a national non-profit conservation organization that helps communities and individuals save working farms, ranches, and forests. Founded in 1980, AFT works to stop the loss of productive farmland and to promote farming practices that lead to a healthy environment and sustainable communities.
1200 18th Street, NW, Suite 800
Washington, DC 20036
Tel: (202) 331-7300
Website: www.farmland.org

Americans for More Civility

A non-partisan, grassroots movement promoting reason, kindness and generosity in public life and private actions. Their website features information about what we all can do to help reduce incivility.

2318 Gathright, Abilene, TX 79606

Website: www.morecivility.com

American Institute of Architects,
Center for Communities by Design

The Center for Livable Communities is the clearinghouse for the AIA's many activities that influence communities' quality of life. The Center is a nonpartisan forum that aims to provide unbiased leadership to facilitate discussions of community design; to partner with other stakeholders to promote innovation; and to inform policy choices for communities, regions, and the nation.

1735 New York Avenue, NW, Washington, DC 20006

Tel: (202) 626-7442

Website: www.aia.org/livable

American Planning Association

APA is a non-profit, public interest organization representing 30,000 practicing planners, elected and appointed officials, and citizens involved in urban and rural planning issues. APA's members believe that sound planning is essential to meeting our nation's economic, environmental, and community development needs.

1776 Massachusetts Ave., NW, Washington, DC 20036-1904

Tel: (202) 872-0611

Website: www.planning.org

America Walks

This is a national coalition of local advocacy groups dedicated to promoting walkable communities. The organization's mission is to foster the development of community-based pedestrian advocacy groups, to educate the public about the benefits of walking, and, when appropriate, to act as a collective voice for walking advocates.

Old City Hall, 45 School Street,
2nd Floor, Boston, MA 02108
Tel: (617) 367-1170
Website: www.americawalks.org

Association of Metropolitan Planning Associations

AMPO was established in 1994 to serve the needs and interests of metropolitan planning organizations (MPOs) nationwide. Federal highway and transit statutes require, as a condition for spending federal highway or transit funds in urbanized areas, the designation of MPOs which have responsibility for planning, programming, and coordination of federal highway and transit investments. MPOs have a strong interest in applying smart growth-type principles to better coordinate transportation planning with local development decision-making.

1730 Rhode Island Avenue, N.W., Suite 608
Washington, DC 20036
Tel: (202) 296-7051
Website: www.ampo.org

Center for Neighborhood Technology

Founded in 1978, CNT develops tools and methods for sustainable development. It has led the way in using transit-oriented development as a redevelopment strategy in urban settings, and it has created a financial intermediary to promote inner-city commercial development around transit.

2125 W North Ave.,
Chicago, IL 60647
Tel: (773) 278-4800
Website: www.cnt.org

The Center for a New American Dream

This organization helps Americans consume responsibly to protect the environment, enhance quality of life, and promote social justice. If you are looking for ways to cut down on television's impact in your life, these folks have plenty of suggestions for that and more.

6930 Carroll Avenue, Suite 900, Takoma Park, MD 20912
Tel: (301) 891-3683 or 1-877-68-DREAM
Website: www.newdream.org

Character Development Group

It is the belief of the CDG that schools can't solve all of the problems which have undermined our students' values. However, through character education, teachers can play a vital role not only in developing better students, but in developing better people. CDG is designed to facilitate this process.

P.O. Box 9211, Chapel Hill, NC 27515-9211
Tel: (919) 967-2110
Website: www.charactereducation.com

Character Education Partnership

The CEP is a non-partisan coalition of organizations and individuals dedicated to developing moral character and civic virtue in our nation's youth as one means of creating a more compassionate and responsible society.

1025 Connecticut Avenue NW, Suite 1011
Washington, DC 20036
Tel: 1-800-988-8081
Website: www.character.org.

Civic Practices Network

CPN is a collaborative and nonpartisan project bringing together a diverse array of organizations and perspectives within the civic renewal movement. CPN members are grassroots environmentalists, business people, and civil servants working

collaboratively to create safe and sustainable local economies.
Center for Human Resources
Heller School for Advanced Studies in Social Welfare,
Brandeis University, 60 Turner Street, Waltham, MA 02154
Tel: (617) 736-4890
Website: www.cpn.org

Cohousing Association of the United States

This organization supports the hundreds of built and forming
cohousing communities across the country. They publish
Cohousing, chronicling the movement's progress, sharing suc-
cesses, and learning from experience. The definitive resource
for information about cohousing in the US.
Website: www.cohousing.org

College Town Life

This organization works to preserve walkable, affordable neighborhoods adjacent to college and university campuses. Before
there was New Urbanism there had to be old urbanism, and
American college towns are prime examples of the livability
and community that once was the norm all over the country.
E-mail: editor@collegetownlife.com
Website: www.collegetownlife.com or
www.users.muohio.edu/karrowrs/college

Communitarian Network

The Communitarian Network grew as a response to a number
of academicians and social commentators noticing a breakdown
in the moral fabric of society. Attributing this condition to an
excessive emphasis on individualism, they recognized the
need for a social philosophy that protected individual rights
while also re-establishing a sense of responsibility to community.
2130 H Street, NW, Suite 703, Washington, DC 20052
Tel: (202) 994-7997
Website: www.gwu.edu/~ccps/

Congress for New Urbanism
   CNU is a collaboration of professionals working to reform
   North America's urban growth patterns. CNU encourages
   restoration of existing urban centers, reconfiguration of
   sprawling suburbs into communities of real neighborhoods
   and diverse districts, conservation of natural environments,
   and preservation of the built legacy.
   5 Third Street, #725, San Francisco, CA 94103
   Tel: (415) 495-2255
   Website: www.cnu.org

Etiquette Consultants for Business
   A small business designed to help combat the growing prob-
   lem of rudeness in the workplace.
   P.O. Box 290116, Columbia, SC 29229
   Tel: (803) 736-1934
   Website: www.eticon.com

Growth Management Leadership Alliance
   Established in 1988, GMLA is a federation of 26 regional and
   state conservation and planning organizations. GMLA is dedicated to heightening the awareness of land use planning as a
   policy tool to address resource conservation, housing, transportation, and key public concerns. Member organizations
   concentrate on issues of development and planning, environmental concerns, and smart growth.
   South Carolina Coastal Conservation League
   P.O. Box 1765, Charleston, SC 29402
   Tel: (843) 723-8035;
   Website: www.scccl.org

International City/County Management Association
   Founded in 1914, ICMA is the professional and educational
   association for more than 8,000 appointed administrators and
   assistant administrators serving cities, counties, other local

governments, and regional entities around the world. ICMA is also the organizational home for the Smart Growth Network, an independent membership organization that assists its members in identifying strategies and tools to protect the health and welfare of their communities through the integration of environmentally sound decision making and economic growth.
777 North Capitol Street, NE, Suite 500
Washington, DC 20002
Tel: (202) 962-3582;
Website: http://icma.org

Local Government Commission

The LGC is a 20-year-old non-profit membership organization that offers education, training, and technical assistance to local areas seeking to implement innovative long-term solutions that further economically and environmentally sustainable land use patterns.
1414 K St., Suite 250, Sacramento, CA 95814
Tel: (916) 448-1198
Website: www.lgc.org

Local Initiatives Support Corporation

LISC helps resident-led, community-based development organizations transform distressed communities and neighborhoods into healthy ones — good places to live, do business, work, and raise families. By providing capital, technical expertise, training, and information, LISC supports the development of local leadership and the creation of affordable housing, commercial, industrial and community facilities, businesses and jobs. They help neighbors build communities.
1825 K Street, Suite 1100, Washington, DC 20006
Tel: (202) 785-2908
Website: www.liscnet.org

The Mayors' Institute on City Design
This program is dedicated to improving the design and livability of America's cities through the efforts of their chief elected leaders. The program is an initiative of the National Endowment for the Arts, established by the NEA in 1986 and now administered by the American Architectural Foundation in partnership with the NEA and the US Conference of Mayors. 1620 Eye Street NW, Third Floor, Washington, DC 20006-4005; Tel: (202) 463-1390; Website: www.micd.org

National Association of Counties
NACo is a full-service organization that provides legislative, research, technical, and public affairs assistance to its members. The association acts as a liaison with other levels of government, works to improve public understanding of counties, serves as a national advocate for counties, and provides counties with resources to help them find innovative methods to meet the challenges they face.
440 First Street, NW, 8th Floor, Washington, DC 20001
Tel: (202) 661-8805
Website: www.naco.org

National Neighborhood Coalition
NNC promotes a neighborhood focus at all levels of government and throughout society by advocating for programs and policies that foster partnerships between neighborhood organizations, private sector institutions, and government agencies.
1221 Connecticut Ave., 2nd Floor
Washington, DC 20036-2628
Tel: (202) 429-0790
Website: www.neighborhoodcoalition.org

National Resources Defense Council
NRDC is a nonprofit organization with more than 400,000 members nationwide. Its mission is to preserve the environment,

protect the public health, and ensure the conservation of wilderness and natural resources. NRDC pursues these goals through research, advocacy, litigation, and public education. NRDC is working in partnership with the Surface Transportation Policy Project and the EPA to develop a tool kit for smart growth. The tool kit includes *Once There Were Greenfields*, a meticulously researched and documented book about sprawl, its impacts, and smart growth alternatives.
40 West 20th Street, New York, NY
Tel: (212) 727-2700
Website: www.nrdc.org

National Town Builders Association

The NTBA is designed to serve builders and developers throughout the nation in an effort to create the very best traditional neighborhoods and town centers. The group is made up of town builders committed to the successful development of smart growth neighborhoods that are economically, socially, and environmentally sustainable.
3220 N Street NW #238, Washington, DC 20007
Tel: (202) 333-1902
Website: www.ntba.net

National Trust for Historic Preservation

Chartered by Congress in 1949, the National Trust has more than 200,000 members and six regional offices to help communities preserve their heritage. The trust promotes downtown revitalization as a major alternative to sprawl through its National Main Street Center as well as through public policy advocacy, conferences, and technical assistance. It has published several books describing techniques for minimizing sprawl and promoting smart growth.
1785 Massachusetts Ave., NW, Washington, DC 20036
Tel: (202) 588-6000
Website: www.nationaltrust.org

New Urban News

A professional newsletter for planners, developers, architects, builders, public officials, and others who are interested in the creation of human-scale communities.

P.O. Box 6515, Ithaca, NY 14851

Tel: (607) 275-3087

Website: www.newurbannews.com

NewUrbanism.org

This organization's purpose is to provide useful information to the general public about urbanism, livable communities, sustainable transportation, sprawl, and how to improve everyone's quality of life. They also provide a list of professionals who practice New Urbanism, as well as an extensive bookstore and many valuable links to other organizations.

615 King Street, Suite 103, Alexandria, VA 22314

Tel: (703) 549-6296

Website: www.newurbanism.org

Partners for Livable Communities

Partners for Livable Communities is a non-profit leadership organization working to improve the livability of communities by promoting quality of life, economic development, and social equity. Since its founding in 1977, Partners has helped communities set a common vision for the future, discover and use new resources for community and economic development, and build public-private coalitions to further their goals.

1429 21st Street, NW, Washington, DC 20036

Tel: (202) 887-5990

Website: www.livable.org

Rails-to-Trails Conservancy

This is the largest trails organization in the country and the only one devoted to converting unused railroad lines to multi-use trails. Since 1986, Rails-to-Trails Conservancy has provided leadership, technical assistance, education, and advocacy to and for its 100,000 members in their quest to preserve a piece of America's railroad heritage as a legacy for future generations.

1100 Seventh Street, NW, 10th Floor, Washington, DC 20036
Tel: (202) 331-9696
Website: www.railtrails.org

Scenic America

Founded in 1978, Scenic America is a national nonprofit membership organization dedicated to preserving and enhancing the scenic character of communities. It promotes scenic conservation by providing individuals and communities nationwide with technical assistance on scenic byways, place-sensitive road design, transportation policies, sign control, and other scenic conservation issues and by educating Congress and state legislatures on site-specific projects in various states. In addition, it produces a full range of publications on preserving the scenic beauty, open space, and quality of life that contribute to the environment and economy.

801 Pennsylvania Ave., SE, Suite 300, Washington, DC 20003
Tel: (202) 543-6200
Website: www.scenic.org

Smart Growth America

Smart Growth America is a coalition of nearly 100 advocacy organizations that have a stake in how metropolitan expansion affects our environment, quality of life, and economic sustainability. The diverse coalition partners include national, state, and local groups working on behalf of the environment, historic preservation, social equity, land conservation, neighborhood redevelopment, farmland protection, labor, town planning, and more.

1200 18th Street NW, Suite 801, Washington, DC 20036
Tel: (202) 207-3351
Website: www.smartgrowthamerica.org

Smart Growth Online

The SGO was founded in 1996 as an amalgamation of planning, environmental, government, and citizen groups to raise public awareness about how growth can improve quality of life. The network generates a comprehensive clearinghouse of up-to-date insights into what's happening with urban growth all over the world.

Sustainable Communities Network, c/o CONCERN
1794 Columbia Rd, NW, Washington, DC 20009
Website: www.smartgrowth.org

Surface Transportation Policy Project

STPP is a coalition of more than 200 organizations working to ensure that transportation policies and investments conserve energy, protect environmental and aesthetic quality, strengthen the economy, promote social equity, and make communities more livable. STPP's Quality of Life Campaign strives to focus media attention and public debate on transportation issues so that communities realize the impact that their transportation systems and land use policies will have on every individual's quality of life.

1100 17th St., NW, 10th Floor,
Washington, DC 20036
Tel: (202) 466-2636
Website: www.transact.org

Sustainable Communities Network

The mission of SCN is to connect individuals and organizations nationwide to the resources they need to help make their communities environmentally sound, socially equitable, and economically prosperous. SCN also manages the website for the Smart Growth Online.

1794 Columbia Road, NW, Washington, DC 20009
Tel: (202) 328-8160
Website: www.sustainable.org

Urban Land Institute

ULI is a nonprofit research and educational institute whose mission is to provide responsible leadership in the use of land in order to enhance the total environment.

1025 Thomas Jefferson Street, NW, Suite 500 West

Washington, DC 20007

Tel: (202) 624-7000

Website: www.uli.org

Walkable Communities

A non-profit organization formed to help places become more walkable and pedestrian friendly. Whether they are large cities, small towns, neighborhoods, business districts, parks, school districts, subdivisions, etc., Walkable Communities works with groups to improve the livability of an area by enhancing its walkability.

320 South Main Street, High Springs, FL 32643

Tel: (386) 454-3304

Website: www.walkable.org

Part Two — Publications

The research for this book spanned almost a decade and includes a voluminous amount of books, articles in periodicals and information from websites. Listed below are the most significant sources if you are interested in further researching the seemingly separate but deeply intertwined subjects of Community, Incivility, Transportation, Urban Planning, and Violence.

Community

Bowling Alone, Robert Putnam, Simon and Schuster, 2000.

The Connection Gap: Why Americans Feel So Alone, Laura Pappano, Rutgers University Press, 1998.

Hometown Money: How to Enrich Your Community with Local Currency, Paul Glover, Ithaca Money, 1995.

"The Impact of Chain Stores on Community," *The Home Town Advantage*, April 1, 2003, <www.newrules.org>

"Invest in Kids Now, or Pay Later," Judy Mann, *The Washington Post*, July 28, 1999, p. C15.

The New Golden Rule, Amitai Etzioni, Basic Books, 1996.

The Plug-in Drug, Marie Winn, Viking Press, 1977.

"Report Shows Big Rise in Treatment For Depression," Shankar Vedantam, *The Washington Post*, January 9, 2002, p. A1.

A Responsive Society, Amitai Etzioni, Jossey-Bass, 1991.

"Study: US Leads in Mental Illness, Lags in Treatment," Rick Weiss, *The Washington Post*, June 7, 2005, p. A3.

"Why Johnny Can't Feel: Poor Relationships With Adults May Explain Youth Alienation," Laura Sessions Stepp, *The Washington Post*, April 23, 1999, p. C1.

Incivility

"The American Uncivil Wars," John Marks, *US News & World Report*, April 22, 1996.

As Tough as Necessary, Richard L. Curwin and Allen N. Mendler, Association for Supervision and Curriculum Development, 1997.

Civility: Manners, Morals, and the Etiquette of Democracy, Stephen L. Carter, Harper Perennial, 1997.

Elbows off the Table, Napkin in the Lap, No Video Games During Dinner, Carol McD. Wallace, St. Martin's Griffin, 1996.

"Insubordination and Intimidation Signal the End of Decorum in Many Classrooms," Alison Schneider, *Chronicle of Higher Education*, March 27, 1998.

"Manners, Please!," Karen Astrid Larson, *McCall's*, June 2000.

"Promoting a Return to 'Civil Society'," Kevin Merida and Barbara Vobejda, *The Washington Post,* December 15, 1996, p. A1.

Say Please, Say Thank You: The Respect We Owe One Another, Donald McCullough, Perigree Books, 1998.

"Schools Awash in Bad Behavior," Linda Perlstein, *The Washington Post,* July 11, 2001, p. B1.

A Short History of Rudeness, Mark Caldwell, Picador, 1999.

Take Back Your Kids: Confident Parenting in Turbulent Times, William J. Doherty, Sorin Books, 2000.

"Vox Vulgaris," Stephen Goode, *Insight,* December 20, 1999.

"Why Are We So Angry?," Diane Hales, *Parade Magazine,* September 2, 2001.

Why is Everyone so Cranky?, Leslie Charles, Hyperion, 1997.

Transportation

The Age of Asphalt, Richard O. Davies, Lippincott, 1975.

Asphalt Nation, Jane Holtz Kay, Crown Publishers, 1997.

The Decline of Transit, Glenn Yago, Cambridge University Press, 1984.

"The End of Cheap Oil," Colin J. Campbell and Jean H. Laherrère, *Scientific American,* March 1998.

"Energy apocalypse looms as the world runs out of oil," *Sunday Observer* (London), July 26, 1998.

Getting There, Stephen B. Goddard, University of Chicago Press, 1994.

"GMU Professor Urges Commuters to Do the Math," Michelle Boorstein, *The Washington Post,* November 23, 2003, p. C4.

"GOP Plans $71 Billion Rail Bill," Don Phillips, *The Washington Post,* September 7, 2001, p. E4.

The Highway and the City, Lewis Mumford, Mentor Books, 1963.

The Hydrogen Economy, Jeremy Rifkin, Jeremy P. Tarcher/Putnam, 2002.

Superhighway-Superhoax, Helen Leavitt, Doubleday, 1970.

Urban Planning

A Better Place to Live, Philip Langdon, Harper Perennial, 1994.

"Bring Back those New Neighborhoods," *Community Potentials,* Newsletter of Partners for Livable Communities, Spring 1998, Vol. 1, Issue 3.

City Planning in America: Between Promise and Despair, Mary Hommann, Praeger, 1993.

"The Cost of Sprawl," *Rails to Trails,* Spring 2001.

Counterfeit Community, John F. Freie, Rowman & Littlefield, 1998.

"Cows Don't Go To School," *American Farmland,* Spring-Summer 1997.

Crabgrass Frontier: The Suburbanization of the United States, Kenneth T. Jackson, Oxford University Press, 1985.

The Dark Ages: Life in the United States 1945-1960, Marty Jezer, South End Press, 1982.

The Death and Life of Great American Cities, Jane Jacobs, Vintage Books, 1961.

"Farming on the Edge," *American Farmland Trust,* April 2003, <www.farmland.org/farmingontheedge/major_findings.htm>

"For Urban Developers, A Hard Row to Hoe," Neil Irwin, *The Washington Post,* January 13, 2003, p. E1.

The Geography of Nowhere, James Howard Kunstler, Touchstone, 1993.

The Great Good Place, Ray Oldenburg, Marlowe and Company, 1989.

Home from Nowhere, James Howard Kunstler, Touchstone, 1998.

"Makeovers bring new life to old malls," Haya El Nasser, *USA Today,* April 23, 2003, p. 3A.

The National Sprawl Fact Sheet, "The Costs of Sprawl," Sierra Club, 1998.

"Redefining the Gathering Place," *Shopping Center World,* January 1, 1999.

"'Smart Growth Politics," E.J. Dionne Jr., *The Washington Post,* January 15, 1999, p. A29.

"Solving the Suburban Zoning Crisis," *Shopping Center World,* May 1, 2000.

"Solving Sprawl," Carl Pope, Sierra Club, August 6, 2001, <www.sierraclub.org/sprawl/report99/index.asp>

Sprawl Kills: How Blandburbs Steal Your Time, Health and Money, Joel Hirschhorn and Richard E. Killingsworth, Revolution Publishing, 2005.

Suburban Nation: The Rise of Sprawl and the Decline of the American Dream, Andres Duany, Elizabeth Plater-Zyberk, and Jeff Speck, North Point Press, 2000.

"Suburban 'Sprawl' Takes Its Place on the Political Landscape," Todd S. Purdum, *The New York Times,* February 6, 1999.

Suburbia, Philip C. Dolce, Anchor Books, 1976.

Ten Principles for Reinventing America's Suburban Strips, Michael D. Beyard and Michael Pawlukiewicz, The Urban Land Institute, 2001.

The Twentieth Century American City, Jon C. Teaford, Johns Hopkins University Press, 1993.

"Walk/Can't Walk: The way cities and suburbs are developed could be bad for your health," Martha T. Moore, *USA Today,* April 23, 2003, p. 2A.

"What's So Bad About Sprawl?" Lynda McDonnell, *Pioneer Planet,* November 18, 1996, <www.pioneerplanet.com>

"U.S. Voters Tell Suburbia to Slow Down," Molly O'Meara, *The Worldwatch Report,* July 15, 1999.

Violence

The A to Z Encyclopedia of Serial Killers, Harold Schechter, Pocket Books, 1997.

"The Age of Anxiety," Sally Squires, *The Washington Post,* December 19, 2000, Health, p. 19.

Born That Way, William Wright, Alfred A. Knopf, 1998.

"The Crime Conundrum," Michael A. Fletcher, *The Washington Post,* January 16, 2000, p. F1.

"Despite Rhetoric, Violent Crime Climbs," David A. Vise and Lorraine Adams, *The Washington Post,* December 5, 1999, p. A3.

"For Children, An Epidemic of Homicide" Judith Havemann, *The Washington Post,* February 7, 1997, p. A1.

"Major Shootings in Workplace Since 1995," *The Washington Post,* December 27, 2000, p. A4.

Manners and Violence, Ignacio L. Götz, Praeger, 2000.

Mind Hunter: Inside the FBI's Elite Serial Crime Unit, John Douglas and Mark Olshaker, Pocket Star Books, 1995.

"Movie Violence, Still Playing," Michael Massing, *The Washington Post,* July 4, 1999., p. B4.

No Suicide, 2003, <www.nosuicide.com/mythsandfacts.html>

"Number Imprisoned Exceed 2 Million, Justice Dept. Says," *The Washington Post,* April 7, 2003, p. A4.

Stop Teaching Our Kids to Kill, Lt. Col. Dave Grossman and Gloria DeGaetano, Crown Publishers, 1999.

"Suburban Parents Worry about Possible Abductions," Tom Jackman & Brigid Schulte, *The Washington Post,* February 29, 2000, p. B3.

"Television and violence: The scale of the problem and where to go from here," B.S. Centerwall, *The Journal of the American Medical Association,* June 10, 1992.

Understanding and Preventing Violence, Albert J. Reiss, Jr. and Jeffrey A. Roth, National Academy Press, 1993.

Violence Policy Center, June 2000, <www.vpc.org/studies/wgun-count.htm>

"When Children Kill: The Search for Clues," Elizabeth Kastor, *The Washington Post,* March 27, 1998, p. C1.

Notes

Introduction: Overview

1. Michael A. Fletcher, "The Crime Conundrum," *The Washington Post*, January 16, 2000, p. F1.

2. Khiota Therrien, "Gunman Kills 2 at Office in Seattle: Manhunt On," *The Washington Post*, November 4, 1999, p. A1.

3. Michael A. Fletcher, "The Crime Conundrum," *The Washington Post*, January 16, 2000, p. F1.

4. Judith Havemann, "For Children, An Epidemic of Homicide," *The Washington Post*, February 7, 1997, p. A1.

5. Wolf Von Eckardt, *Back to the Drawing Board: Planning for Livable Cities*, Simon and Schuster, 1978, p. 99.

6. Stanley Buder, "The Future of the American Suburb" in *Suburbia*, Philip C. Dolce, ed. Anchor Books, 1976, p. 199–200.

7. Witold Rybczynski, *City Life*, Scribner, 1995, p. 190–192.

8. Sierra Club, "The Costs of Sprawl," *The National Sprawl Fact Sheet*, 1998.

9. Carl Pope, "Solving Sprawl," Sierra Club, August 6, 2001, <www.sierraclub.org/sprawl/report99/index.asp>

10. Edward T. Hall, *The Hidden Dimension,* Anchor Books, 1999, p. 175.

11. Frank J. Coppa, "Cities and Suburbs in Europe and the United States" in *Suburbia,* Philip C. Dolce, ed. Anchor Books, 1976, p. 188.

12. The use of the term "first-world" in most of my comparisons is in no way indicative that developing countries are insignificant. All I am attempting to do is compare apples with apples by lining up America with its so-called first-world peers: nations that have similar economic, political, and legal systems.

Chapter 1: Sprawl vs. Community

1. Linda Wheeler, "Broken Ground, Broken Hearts," *The Washington Post,* June 21, 1999, p. A7.

2. James Howard Kunstler, *The Geography of Nowhere,* Touchstone, 1993, p. 15.

3. Richard J. Jackson and Chris Kocktitzky, *Creating a Healthy Environment,* p. 8–9, <www.sprawlwatch.organization/health.pdf>

4. Steve Twomey, "Lots Not To Like," *The Washington Post,* July 5, 1999, p. C1.

5. Ibid., p. C1.

6. Philip Langdon, *A Better Place to Live,* Harper Perennial, 1994, p. 1.

7. Ray Oldenburg, *The Great Good Place,* Marlowe and Company, 1991, p. 5.

8 Amitai Etzioni, *A Responsive Society,* Jossey-Bass, 1991, p. 140.

9. Edward Thompson Jr. and Timothy W. Warman, "Meeting the Challenge of Farmland Protection in the 21st Century," *American Farmland,* Summer, 2000.

10. "Cows Don't Go to School," *American Farmland,* Spring-Summer 1997, p. 4.

11. James Howard Kunstler, *Home from Nowhere,* Touchstone, 1998, p. 70.

12. "Earth Pulse," *National Geographic,* March 2001.

13. Jeremy Rifkin, *The Hydrogen Economy* Jeremy P. Tarcher/Putnam, 2002, p. 148.

14. Ibid., p. 147.

15. James Howard Kunstler, *Home from Nowhere,* Touchstone, 1998, p. 67–69.

16 Ibid., p. 68–69.

17. Ibid., p. 68-69.

18. Stephen B. Goddard, *Getting There,* University of Chicago Press, 1994, p. 82; and Joel Schwartz, "Evolution of the Suburbs" in *Suburbia,* Philip C. Dolce, ed., Anchor Books, 1976, p. 11.

19 Marty Jezer, *The Dark Ages: Life in the United States 1945-1960,* South End Press, 1982, p. 141.

20. Kenneth T. Jackson, *Crabgrass Frontier,* Oxford University Press, 1985, p. 250.

21. John F. Freie, *Counterfeit Community,* Rowman & Littlefield, 1998, pp. 23, 31.

22. Ibid., pp. 24, 29.

23. Ibid., 1998, pp. 17, 34, 75.

24. Richard L. Curwin and Allen N. Mendler, *As Tough as Necessary,* Association for Supervision and Curriculum Development, 1997, p. 39–40.

25. Paula Span, "Soap And Waterworks," *The Washington Post,* June 26, 1999, p. C5.

26. Liz Langley, "Mad Icon Disease," *Alternet.org,* May 1, 2003, <www.alternet.org>

27. *Screen Digest,* August 1999, <www.screendigest.com>

28. Peter Elmlund, "Street Life," *Axess Magazine,* Issue 1, 2004.

29. Thomas Moore, *Care of the Soul,* Harper Perennial, 1994, p. 92.

30. Mary Hommann, *City Planning in America,* Praeger Publishers, 1993, p. 7.

31. Wolf Von Eckardt, *Back to the Drawing Board: Planning for Livable Cities,* Simon and Schuster, 1978, p. 117–121.

32. Paul Ginsborg, *A History of Contemporary Italy,* Palgrave MacMillan, 2003, p. 280.

33. Wolf Von Eckardt, *Back to the Drawing Board: Planning for Livable Cities,* Simon and Schuster, 1978, p. 30.

34. Craig Wilson, "Good Simplicity Falls by the Wayside," *USA Today,* July 2, 1999, p. 1.

35. Ibid., p. 1.

36. Katherine Salant, "Celebrating the Past in Style," *The Washington Post,* June 26, 1999, p. G5.

37. "New Urban Projects on a Neighborhood Scale in the United States," *New Urban News,* December 2003, <www.newurbannews.com>

38. Haya El Nasser, "Makeovers bring new life to old malls," *USA Today,* April 23, 2003, p. 3A.

Chapter 2: A Society of Strangers

1. Charles J. Holahan, *Environmental Psychology*, McGraw Hill, 1982, pg. 322.

2 Abigail Trafford, "The Healing Power of Friendship," *The Washington Post,* October 3, 2000, Health Section, p. 5.

3. Dalai Lama and Howard C. Cutler, MD, *The Art of Happiness,* Riverhead Books, 1998, p. 70.

4. Laura Pappano, *The Connection Gap: Why Americans Feel So Alone,* Rutgers University Press, 1998, p. 93; Barbara Schneider and David Stevenson, *The Ambitious Generation,* Yale University Press, 2000, p. 93; "Feral and Furious," *The Economist,* November 13, 2004, p. 93; Philip Langdon, *A Better Place to Live,* Harper Perennial, 1994, pp. 20, 24.

5. Thomas Moore, *Care of the Soul,* Harper Perennial, 1992, p. 93.

6. Dr. Edward Shorter, *Doctors and Their Patients: A Social History,* Transaction Publishers, 1991, p. 212–217.

7. Rick Weiss, "Study: US Leads in Mental Illness, Last in Treatment," *Washington Post,* June 7, 2005, p. A3.

8. Sally Squires, "The Age of Anxiety," *The Washington Post,* December 19, 2000, Health Section, p. 19.

9. Shankar Vedantam, "Report Shows Big Rise in Treatment For Depression," *The Washington Post,* January 9, 2002, p. A1.

10. Mariko Thompson, "Moody Blues," *The Washington Times,* November 11, 2003, p. B1.

11. Philip Langdon, *A Better Place to Live,* Harper Perennial, 1994, p. 25.

12. *Centers for Disease Control,* National Center for Injury Prevention and Control. <www.cdc.gov/ncipc/factsheets/suifacts.htm>; *No Suicide.com,* 2003, <www.nosuicide.com/mythsandfacts.html>; Mariko Thompson, "Moody Blues," *The Washington Times,* November 11, 2003, p. B1.

13. Abigail Trafford, "Death in the Morning," *The Washington Post,* June 19, 2001, Health Section, p. 4.

14. Mariko Thompson, "Moody Blues," *The Washington Times,* November 11, 2003, p. B1.

15. Ibid., p. B4.

16. Abigail Trafford, "The Healing Power of Friendship," *The Washington Post,* October 3, 2000, Health Section, p. 5.

17. Molly O'Meara, "U.S. Voters Tell Suburbia to Slow Down," *The Worldwatch Report,* July 15, 1999, p. 1.

18. Philip Langdon, *A Better Place to Live,* Harper Perennial, 1994, p. 25.

19. Dorothy Rich, "Children in Confinement," *The Washington Post,* January 26, 2003, p. B8.

20. Desmond Morris, *The Naked Ape,* Dell, 1967, p. 116.

21. Paul Trout, "Low Marks for Top Teachers," *The Washington Post,* March 13, 2000, p. A17.

22. International Institute for Democracy and Electoral Assistance (IDEA), <www.idea.int/vt/>

23. Anjetta McQueen, "Home alone is norm for many kids," *The Grand Rapids Press,* September 11, 2000, p. A1.

24. Ferenc Maté, *A Reasonable Life,* Albatross Publishing House, 1997, p. 103.

Chapter 3: A Culture of Incivility

1. Edward T. Hall, *Beyond Culture,* Anchor Books, 1981, p. 16.

2. Amitai Etzioni, *The New Golden Rule,* Basic Books, 1996, p. 166.

3. Richard A. Barrett, *Culture and Conduct,* Wadsworth, 1984, p. 61.

4. Ibid., p. 63.

5. Ronald Gross and Paul Osterman, *Individualism: Man in Modern Society,* Dell, 1971, p. xxvii.

6. Stephanie Coontz, *The Way We Never Were,* Basic Books, 2000, p. 69–76.

7. Daniel J. Boorstin, *The Americans: The National Experience,* Random House, 1965, p. 51–54.

8. Diane Hales, "Why Are We So Angry?" *Parade Magazine, September 2, 2001, p. 11.*

9. John Marks, "The American Uncivil Wars," *US News & World Report,* April 22, 1996, p. 66–72.

10. Alison Schneider, "Insubordination and Intimidation Signal the End of Decorum in Many Classrooms," *Chronicle of Higher Education,* March 27, 1998.

11. Linda Perlstein, "Schools Awash in Bad Behavior," *The Washington Post,* July 11, 2001, p. B1.

12. Ibid., p. B1.

13. Sewell Chan, "Motorists Advised to Yield," *The Washington Post,* July 22, 1999, p. DC1.

14. KFMBTV, CBS, Channel 8, San Diego, July 13, 2001, <www2.kfmb.com/special_assignment/archive/2001/02/daring.php>

15. Mark Caldwell, *A Short History of Rudeness,* Picador, 1999, p. 51.

16. Ignacio L. Götz, *Manners and Violence,* Praeger Publishers, 2000, p. 51.

17. Martha Frase-Blunt, "The Jerk at Work: Enough to Make You Sick," *The Washington Post,* March 5, 2002, p. F1.

18. Ibid., p. F5.

19. Michael Massing, "Movie Violence. Still Playing," *The Washington Post,* July 4, 1999, p. B4.

20. Stephen Goode, "Vox Vulgaris," *Insight,* December 20, 1999, p. 10.

21. Ibid., p. 11.

22. Don Oldenburg, "Ads Aimed At Kids," *The Washington Post,* May 3, 2001, p. C4.

23. Conrad Philip Kottak, *Prime-Time Society,* Wadsworth, 1992, p. 3.

24. Ibid., p. 3.

25. Ibid., p. 4.

26. Ibid., p. 198.

27. John F. Freie, *Counterfeit Community,* Rowman & Littlefield, 1998, p. 76.

Chapter 4: A Breeding Ground for Violence

1. "The Experience of Flight," *Popular Science,* November 2003, p. 72.

2. Candy Sagon, "Restaurant Rage," *The Washington Post,* September 5, 2001, p. F1; Jenifer McKim, "Now at the Mall: 'Parking Lot Rage'," *The Washington Post,* January 14, 2001, p. A19.

3. Candy Sagon, "Restaurant Rage," *The Washington Post,* September 5, 2001, p. F6.

4. Ignacio L. Götz, *Manners and Violence,* Praeger Publishers, 2000, pp. ix, 3.

5. Mark Caldwell, *A Short History of Rudeness,* Picador, 1999, p. 48.

6. Judith Havemann, "For Children, an Epidemic of Homicide," *The Washington Post,* February 7, 1997, p. A1.

7. Robert Bassman, "Capitals," *Europe,* April 1994, p. 36.

8. Rob Nelson, *Last Call,* Dell, 2000, p. 122.

9. Lt. Col. Dave Grossman and Gloria DeGaetano, *Stop Teaching Our Kids to Kill,* Crown Publishers, 1999, pp. 14, 15.

10. Ibid., p. 14.

11. Harold Schechter, *The A to Z Encyclopedia of Serial Killers,* Pocket Books, 1996/1997, p. 276.

12. Ibid., p. 276.

13. Tom Knowles, interview by author, April 12, 2001; Centers for Disease Control and Prevention, *Sexual Violence Fact Sheet,* <www.cdc.gov/ncipc/factsheets/svfacts.htm> and US Department of Justice, *Rape and Sexual Assault 1997,* <www. ojp.gov/ovc/ncvrw/1999/rape.htm>; Project Sister, "Are You Aware?," <www.projectsister.org>; Carrie Donovan, "Women Under Siege," *The Washington Post,* April 18, 2000, Health Section, p. 31.

14. Blain Harden, "The Banality of Gary: A Green River Chiller," *The Washington Post,* November 16, 2003, p. D6.

15. Laura Sessions Step, "Why Johnny Can't Feel: Poor Relationships With Adults May Explain Youth Alienation," *The Washington Post,* April 23, 1999, p. C1.

16. John Douglas and Mark Olshaker, *Mind Hunter: Inside the FBI's Elite Serial Crime Unit,* Pocket Star Books, 1995, p. 364.

17. Richard L. Curwin and Allen N. Mendler, *As Tough as Necessary,* Association for Supervision and Curriculum Development, 1997, p. 40.

18. Elizabeth Kastor, "When Children Kill: The Search for Clues," *The Washington Post,* March 27, 1998, p. C1.

19. Michael Massing, "Movie Violence. Still Playing," *The Washington Post,* July 4, 1999, p. B4.

20. B.S. Centerwall, "Television and violence: the scale of the problem and where to go from here," *Journal of the American Medical Association,* June 10, 1992.

21. Michael Massing, "Movie Violence. Still Playing," *The Washington Post,* July 4, 1999, p. B4.

22. Rob Stein, "Suburbia USA: Fat of the Land?" *The Washington Post,* August 29, 2003, p. A3.

Chapter 5: Creating a More Fulfilling Life

1. Anjetta McQueen, "Home alone is norm for many kids," *The Grand Rapids Press,* September 11, 2000, p. A1.

2. Judy Mann, "Invest in Kids Now, or Pay Later," *The Washington Post,* July 28, 1999, p. C15.

3. Don Morgan, "Federal Role in Schools Expands Despite GOP Misgivings," *The Washington Post,* October 23, 2000, p. A2.

4. "20 Ways to Use Your Money for a Better World," *Co-op America Quarterly,* Fall 2003, p. 13.

5. Ibid., p. 14.

6. USDA, "Farmer's Market Facts," April, 2003, <www.ams.usda. gov/farmersmarkets/facts.htm>

7. William Claiborne, "Fighting the 'New Feudal Rulers'," *The Washington Post,* January 3, 1999, p. A3.

8. Stacy Mitchell, "Shoppers Urged to Break Free of Chains," *The Home Town Advantage,* November 23, 2004, <www. newrules.org/retail>

9. "Inside Seaside," *The Washington Post,* January 29, 2004, p. H3.

10. Marie Winn, *The Plug-in Drug,* Viking Press, 1977, p. 23–25.

11. Ibid., p. 23–25.

12. Ibid., p. 23–25.

13. Ibid., p. 23–25.

Chapter 6: Creating a Healthier Society

1. John F. Freie, *Counterfeit Community*, Rowman & Littlefield, 1998, p. 186.

2. Alan K. Simpson and Richard D. Lamm, "571 Million Americans," *The Washington Post*, June 20, 2000, p. A23.

3. E.J. Dionne Jr., "'Smart Growth' Politics," *The Washington Post*, January 15, 1999, p. A29.

4. Mary Hommann, *City Planning in America*, Praeger, 1993, p. 14.

5. Steve Bergsmann, "Cultivating a Global Village," *Shopping Center World*, May 1999.

6. Stanley Buder, "The Future of the American Suburb," in *Suburbia*, Phillip C. Dolce, ed., Anchor Books, 1976, p. 211.

7. Ibid., p. 212; Wolf Von Eckardt, *Back to the Drawing Board: Planning for Livable Cities*, Simon and Schuster, 1978, p. 151.

8. Wolf Von Eckardt, *Back to the Drawing Board: Planning for Livable Cities*, Simon and Schuster, 1978, p. 127–131.

9. Ibid., p. 151–152.

10. Lori Montgomery, "Glendening Named Head of Smart Growth Institute," *The Washington Post*, February 11, 2003, p. B1.

11. Mary Hommann, *City Planning in America*, Praeger, 1993, p. 1.

12. Michael D. Beyard and Michael Pawlukiewicz, *Ten Principles for Reinventing America's Suburban Strips*, The Urban Land Institute, 2001, p. 8–9.

13. Don Phillips, "Mounting Congestion Is Challenging to DOT," *The Washington Post*, May 15, 2001, p. A15.

14. Glenn Yago, *The Decline of Transit*, Cambridge University Press, 1984, p. 195.

15. James Carnahan, "Where's the Vision," *Trains,* July 1998, p. 72.

16. Don Phillips, "Amtrak: The Boost that Began Sept. 11 May Not Be Temporary," *The Washington Post,* September 23, 2001, p. H6.

17. Don Phillips, "GOP Plans $71 Billion Rail Bill," *The Washington Post,* September 7, 2001, p. E1.

18. Glenn Yago, *The Decline of Transit,* Cambridge University Press, 1984, p. 204.

19. Steven Pearlstein, "From Greenspan: No Fear of Oil Heights," *The Washington Post,* October 17, 2004, p. F2; Mark Hertsgaard, "Running on Empty," *The Washington Post,* June 13, 2004, p. 6; Jeremy Rifkin, *The Hydrogen Economy,* Jeremy P. Tarcher/Putnam, 2002, p. 28; "Energy apocalypse looms as the world runs out of oil," *Sunday Observer* (London), July 26, 1998; Colin J. Campbell and Jean H. Laherrère, "The End of Cheap Oil," *Scientific American,* March 1998.

20. "Earth Pulse," *National Geographic,* March 2001.

21. Joel Schwartz, "Evolution of the Suburbs," in *Suburbia,* Philip C. Dolce, ed., Anchor Books, 1976, p. 29.

22. American Farmland Trust, "Farming on the Edge," April 2003, <www.farmland.org/farmingontheedge/major_findings.htm>

23. Judith Haverman, "Gore Proposal Aims to Tame Urban Sprawl," *The Washington Post,* January 11, 1999, p. A2.

24. Todd S. Purdum, "Suburban 'Sprawl' Takes Its Place on the Political Landscape," *The New York Times,* February 6, 1999.

25. Kenneth T. Jackson, *Crabgrass Frontier,* Oxford University Press, 1985, p. 294.

26. International Institute for Democracy and Electoral Assistance, <www.idea.int/vt/index.cfm>

Chapter 7: A Vision for a Better Future

1. Brad Wolverton, "Building a New Trust," *The Chronicle of Philanthropy*, November 13, 2003, p. 23.

Appendix A: How Sprawl Came to Be

1. Daniel J. Boorstin, *The Americans: The Democratic Experience*, Vintage Books, 1973, p. 261–2.

2. Stephen B. Goddard, *Getting There*, University of Chicago Press, 1994, p. 9.

3. Ibid., p. 11.

4. Ibid., p. 14.

5. Ibid., p. 64.

6. Richard O. Davies, *The Age of Asphalt*, Lippincott, 1975, p. 10.

7. Ibid., p. 11.

8. Joel Schwartz, "Evolution of the Suburbs," in *Suburbia*, Philip C. Dolce, ed., Anchor Books, 1976, p. 24.

9. Helen Leavitt, *Superhighway-Superhoax*, Doubleday, 1970, p. 23–25.

10. Stephen B. Goddard, *Getting There*, University of Chicago Press, 1994, p. 166.

11. Kenneth T. Jackson, *Crabgrass Frontier*, Oxford University Press, 1985, p. 250.

12. Lewis Mumford, *The Highway and the City*, Mentor Books, 1963, p. 134.

13. Kenneth T. Jackson, "The Effect of Suburbanization on Cities," in *Suburbia*, Philip C. Dolce, ed., Anchor Books, 1976,. p. 102.

14. Kenneth T. Jackson, *Crabgrass Frontier,* Oxford University Press, 1985, p. 272.

15. Margaret S. Marsh and Samuel Kaplan, "The Lure of the Suburbs," in *Suburbia,* Philip C. Dolce, ed., Anchor Books, 1976, p. 40.

16. Joel Schwartz, "Evolution of the Suburbs," in *Suburbia,* Philip C. Dolce, ed., Anchor Books, 1976, p. 10.

17. Stephen B. Goddard, *Getting There,* University of Chicago Press, 1994, p. 67–68.

18. Kenneth T. Jackson, "The Effects of Suburbanization on the Cities," in *Suburbia,* Philip C. Dolce, ed., Anchor Books, 1976, p. 100.

19. Stephen B. Goddard, *Getting There,* University of Chicago Press, 1994, p. 126.

20. Jon C. Teaford, *The Twentieth Century American City,* 1993, p. 66.

21. Kenneth T. Jackson, *Crabgrass Frontier,* Oxford University Press, 1985, p. 168.

22. Daniel Yergin, *The Prize: The Epic Quest for Oil, Money, and Power,* Simon and Schuster, 1991, p. 79.

23. Lewis Mumford, *The Highway and the City,* Mentor Books, 1963, p. 252–253.

24. Stephen B. Goddard, *Getting There,* University of Chicago Press, 1994, p. 126.

25. Ibid., p. 129.

26. Edward W. Miller, "Getting There: Light Rail," *The Coastal Report,* September 1999, p. 1.

27. Glenn Yago, *The Decline of Transit,* Cambridge University Press, 1984, p. 64.

28. Marty Jezer, *The Dark Ages: Life in the United States 1945-1960,* South End Press, 1982, p. 141.

29. Stephen B. Goddard, *Getting There,* University of Chicago Press, 1994, p. 82; and Joel Schwartz, "Evolution of the Suburbs" in *Suburbia,* Philip C. Dolce, ed. Anchor Books, 1976, p. 11.

30. Ibid., p. 142.

31. Ibid., pp. 139, 140.

32. Kenneth T. Jackson, *Crabgrass Frontier,* Oxford University Press, 1985, p. 208.

33. Ibid., p. 215; James Howard Kunstler, *The Geography of Nowhere,* Touchstone, 1993, p. 104.

34. Marty Jezer, *The Dark Ages: Life in the United States 1945-1960,* South End Press, 1982, p. 120.

35. Ibid., p. 185; Kenneth T. Jackson, *Crabgrass Frontier,* Oxford University Press, 1985, p. 217.

36. Witold Rybczynski, *City Life,* Scribner, 1995, p. 160.

37. Marty Jezer, *The Dark Ages: Life in the United States 1945-1960,* South End Press, 1982, p. 185.

38. Stephen B. Goddard, *Getting There,* University of Chicago Press, 1994, p. 184.

39. Lewis Mumford, *The Highway and the City,* Mentor Books, 1963, p. 247.

40. Helen Leavitt, *Superhighway-Superhoax,* Doubleday, 1970, p. 52.

41. Stephen B. Goddard, *Getting There,* University of Chicago Press, 1994, p. 217.

42. Mary Hommann, *City Planning in America,* Praeger, 1993, p. 7.

Appendix B: Sprawl Raises Local Taxes

1. Sierra Club, "The Costs of Sprawl," *The National Sprawl Fact Sheet,* 1998.

2. Charles Lockwood, "Creating Sprawl," *Environmental News Network,* October 28, 1999, <www.enn.com>

3. Sierra Club, "The Costs of Sprawl," *The National Sprawl Fact Sheet,* 1998.

4. Charles Lockwood, "Creating Sprawl," *Environmental News Network,* October 28, 1999, <www.enn.com>

5. Sierra Club, "The Costs of Sprawl," *The National Sprawl Fact Sheet,* 1998.

6. Lynda McDonnell, "What's So Bad About Sprawl?" *Pioneer Planet,* November 18, 1996, <www.pioneerplanet.com>

7. Sierra Club, "The Costs of Sprawl," *The National Sprawl Fact Sheet,* 1998.

Index

Sierra Club, 9, 17, 53, 159,
215, 219, 220, 234
Simon, Robert E. Jr., 126
Slepian, Anne, 101
slums, 36, 190, 191
small towns, 1, 5, 7, 9, 32, 33,
36, 47, 48, 64, 88, 91, 108-
113, 123-126, 129, 131,
132, 137, 138, 147, 148,
150-153, 155, 156, 160,
161, 170, 174, 176, 185,
196, 211, 244
fake, 41-43
living in, 32, 40, 109
smart growth, 41, 126, 201,
204, 207, 215, 229
Smart Growth America, 209
Smart Growth Leadership
Institute, 130
Smart Growth Online, 210
Smith, Adam, 27
Solanas, Valerie, 104
Sprague, Frank J., 180
sprawl, 16-23
expense of, 23-27
history of, 37, 165-196
Standard Oil, 128, 183
Stevenson, David, 50, 223
stores, local, *see* local stores
streetcars, 12, 175, 180, 181,
183, 186, 224
see also trolleys
suicide, 50, 51, 216, 223
see also depression;
isolation; loneliness
Surface Transportation Policy
Project, 207, 210
Sustainable Communities
Network, 210

T
Tangires, Helen, ii
tax laws and sprawl, 30, 124,
152-155, 157
taxes, local, 23, 24, 197, 234
television
as addiction, 114-115
and community, 32, 33, 34,
57, 76, 90, 115-117, 163,
202
and culture, 65, 72, 73, 88,
113, 114, 116
as a drug, 115, 115, 117,
162
and rudeness, 75-76
and violence, 79, 88, 89, 90,
97, 217, 227
see also culture, condition of
third place, 22
Thoreau, Henry David, 150
Toronto, 36, 37, 50
traditional neighborhood
developments, 41, 126, 151
traffic, 17, 26, 37, 54, 57, 77, 78,
119, 135, 138, 140-143, 184
see also gridlock
transit-oriented development,
28, 41, 126, 205
see also mass transit; public
transport
transportation, diversified, 10,
139, 145
trolleys, 26-29, 132, 133, 138-
140, 162, 170-172, 175,
180-185
see also streetcars
Trujillo, Laura, 70
TV addiction, *see* television as
addiction

About the Author

INTERNATIONAL ENTREPRENEUR, magazine columnist, and published author of five books, Doug Morris spent over 14 years living in the safe, community-oriented cities and towns of Canada and Europe. Upon returning to the US he was stunned at the extensive urban decay, lack of livable small towns, and comparatively non-existent public transit and passenger rail systems. This prompted him to begin a twenty-year search for the livable places in the United States. He visited streetcar, railroad, and garden suburbs; college towns, urban neighborhoods, greenbelt villages, strip malls, and every place in between. Though he did find some locations with a semblance of community life, the author's quest confirmed that genuine communities, and the safety they confer, were extremely rare in the US.

Mr. Morris then combined his extensive international experience and multi-cultural perspective with over eight years of in-depth study and research to uncover the negative sociological, cultural and personal impacts of sprawl. The result of which is this book, designed to ameliorate the twin problems of suburban sprawl and urban blight, while also helping each individual American find the safety and sense of belonging that comes from being a part of a genuine community.

For more information about Doug and his work, please visit www.ItsaSprawlWorld.com.

Other New Society Publishers titles of interest

Toward Sustainable Communities
Resources for Citizens and Their Governments

Mark Roseland,
Foreword by Jeb Brugmann

Local governments are increasingly caught between rising expectations that development initiatives be sustainable and the fact that more and more services are being downloaded to the municipal level. The third edition of this classic text offers practical suggestions and innovative solutions to a range of community problems, including energy efficiency, transportation, land use, housing, waste reduction, recycling, air quality and governance. In clear language, with updated tools, initiatives and resources, a new preface and foreword, this sustainable practices-resource is for both citizens and governments.

Mark Roseland is director of the Centre for Sustainable Community Development at Simon Fraser University in British Columbia.

256 pages 8 x 9" Pb ISBN 0-86571-535-1 US$22.95 / Can$29.95

Better Not Bigger
How to Take Control of Urban Growth and Improve Your Community

Eben Fodor

Better NOT Bigger provides insights, ideas, and tools to empower citizens to switch off their local "growth machine" by debunking the pro-growth rhetoric. Highly accessible to ordinary citizens as well as professional planners.
"A manual for taking apart the machinery of hidden policies and political coalitions that drive unfettered growth in our towns and cities. Buy this book. Take it home. Read it. Then pass it on." — Alan Durning

184 pages 5.5 x 8.5" ISBN 0-86571-386-3 US$15.95 / Can$19.95

The Natural Step for Communities

How Cities and Towns can Change to Sustainable Practices

Sarah James & Torbjörn Lahti

This book provides inspiring examples of 60+ eco-municipalities that have made dramatic changes toward sustainability — towns like Övertorneå, whose government operations recently became 100 per cent fossil fuel-free — and explains how others can emulate their success. It argues that an integrated approach can surmount challenges of conflicting priorities, scarce resources and turf battles. It also clarifies the concept of sustainability, offering guiding principles from the Natural Step framework.

304 pages 7.5 x 9" 100 B&W Photos
ISBN 0-86571-491-6   Pb US$24.95 / Can$29.95

The Key to Sustainable Cities

Meeting Human Needs, Transforming Community Systems

Gwendolyn Hallsmith

Despite wide agreement on the core values of sustainable societies, municipalities are so busy solving current problems they don't have the time or resources to plan effective action for sustainability. The Key to Sustainable Cities uses the principles of system dynamics to demon-

strate how today's problems were yesterday's solutions. The book points to a new approach to city planning that builds on assets as a starting point for cities to develop healthy social, governance, economic and environmental systems.

272 pages 6 x 9" Pb ISBN 0-86571-499-1 US$19.95 / Can$27.95

If you have enjoyed *Its a Sprawl World After All*,
you might also enjoy other

BOOKS TO BUILD A NEW SOCIETY

Our books provide positive solutions for people who want to
make a difference. We specialize in:

**Environment and Justice • Conscientious Commerce
Sustainable Living • Ecological Design and Planning
Natural Building & Appropriate Technology • New Forestry
Educational and Parenting Resources • Nonviolence
Progressive Leadership • Resistance and Community**

New Society Publishers

ENVIRONMENTAL BENEFITS STATEMENT

New Society Publishers has chosen to produce this book on Enviro 100, recycled paper
made with **100% post consumer waste**, processed chlorine free, and old growth
free.

For every 5,000 books printed, New Society saves the following resources:[1]

31	Trees
2,772	Pounds of Solid Waste
3,050	Gallons of Water
3,978	Kilowatt Hours of Electricity
5,039	Pounds of Greenhouse Gases
22	Pounds of HAPs, VOCs, and AOX Combined
8	Cubic Yards of Landfill Space

---

[1] Environmental benefits are calculated based on research done by the Environmental Defense Fund and
other members of the Paper Task Force who study the environmental impacts of the paper industry.

For more information on this environmental benefits statement, or to inquire about environmentally
friendly papers, please contact New Leaf Paper – info@newleafpaper.com Tel: 888 • 989 • 5323.

For a full list of NSP's titles, please call **1-800-567-6772** *or check out our website at:*

www.newsociety.com

NEW SOCIETY PUBLISHERS